P9-CQT-462

DR. DAVID R. MILLER

Christian
Parenting
B O O K S

Unless otherwise specified, Scripture quotations are from the *Holy Bible: New International Version* ©1973, 1978, 1984 by International Bible Society. Used by permission of Zondervan Bible Publishers.

Christian Parenting Books is an imprint of Chariot Family Publishing, a div. of David C. Cook Publishing Co.
David C. Cook Publishing Co., Elgin, Illinois 60120
David C. Cook Publishing Co., Weston, Ontario
Nova Distribution Ltd., Newton Abbot, England

TOUGH KIDS
©1993 by David Miller

All rights reserved. Except for brief excerpts for review purposes, no part of this book may be reproduced or used in any form without written permission from the publisher.

Cover design by Foster Design Associates
Editing and Interior Design by Advent Communications

First Printing, 1993
Printed in the United States of America
97 96 95 94 93 5 4 3 2 1

CIP Applied for.
ISBN 0-78140-939-X

For Laurie,
Who will always be loved.

Table of Contents

Introduction

Tough Kids! Some may think such a term unkind, and it may be somewhat too strong in some cases. My use of this phrase, however, is based on the words I hear from parents who come to me for counsel. I don't hear terms such as "failed to bond," "unattached," or "destructive." Parents don't talk this way because they see the problem from inside the family, through the eyes of love and optimism that characterize the majority of challenged parents.

This book focuses on a variety of child and adolescent problems. Some are developmental in nature while others may be traced to prematurity, early abuse or neglect or even mental illness. Some may be due to poor parenting practices while some children are "tough" for unknown reasons.

I am writing as a licensed child and adolescent therapist *and* as a parent of a tough child. What my wife and I learned allowed us to go from being mere survivors to overcomers, enabled to continue doing our best for our own tough kid in the face of the darkest days imaginable. We've learned that children are only on loan to parents and must someday be returned to God. We've learned that *our* children are really *His* children, trusted to our care for a few years and then released to follow the path He has laid out before them.

The case studies you will read are true, though the names and places have been changed for obvious reasons. I welcome you to my family and to the families of tough kids with whom I've worked over the years. I believe that what I have to share can help maintain the sanity of all kinds of parents, but particularly Christian parents who seem to struggle more with guilt and embarrassment and often see a tough kid as God's way of punishing them.

No one needs application of 2 Timothy 1:7 more than challenged parents. "For God has not given us a spirit of fear, but of power, and of love and of self-discipline."

1

Why Us, Lord?

It is 8:45 on a Sunday morning and the Kravchuk family is getting ready for church. Jeff and Elaine are up in their bedroom putting on the finishing touches. Their nine-year-old son, Billy, is in his room trying to get the milk and cereal stains off his Sunday shirt before mom notices. Jennifer, 11, is waiting impatiently downstairs—and no one notices that seven-year-old Darrell is not around.

On the way home from church, Jeff notices what seems to be a cat lying in the road by their house. Not wanting to alarm his kids, he says nothing. While Elaine is preparing dinner, he walks down the street and sure enough, the family cat, "Boots," is lying dead in the road.

"Funny," Jeff thinks, "It doesn't really look like Boots was run over."

It will be two years before Jeff and Elaine Kravchuk learn that Boots was just another victim of Darrell's often uncontrollable anger. Discovering the extent of their young son's "problem" will come after another family cat is found dead.

This time, however, a neighbor will see Darrell strangle it, and call the police.

Only when their nine year old is evaluated in a psychiatric unit for children, will the full horror of Darrell's behavior come to light: abusing younger neighborhood children, torturing and killing pets from other families, starting fires in the area—nearly unbelievable stories were surfacing.

As Jeff and Elaine Kravchuk sat in my office, a feeling of disgrace and confusion seemed to emanate from their very beings. These parents were struggling valiantly to understand what was happening to their family. Darrell was ten years old by now, and the experts had told the Kravchuks that their son might never recover from whatever is bothering him. Worse yet, for there to be any chance at recovery, Darrell will have to live away from his family for an extended period of time— maybe even years!

Is Darrell's problem their fault? Had Jeff and Elaine Kravchuk committed some terrible abuse on their son without knowing it? Was Darrell the tool of God's judgement on them for past sins? Or was there another answer?

Across town, another Christian family was experiencing their own problem child. They faced a very different situation, but it felt no less severe for the family going through it.

Bob and Jill Lunton had been childless for the first nine years of their marriage. Jill had always felt she was "born" to be a mother, so she'd been distraught to discover she was unable to conceive and bear children. They'd seen every specialist in the area, and knew their case was hopeless.

Bob and Jill decided to adopt a child or two through an overseas adoption agency. They had seen television commercials depicting horrendous living conditions in several Central American countries, and applied to adopt a child from Costa Rica.

Juan was five when he stepped off the plane and into the Lunton family. Only five—and looking even younger. Obviously hunger and deprivation had taken a toll on his young body, but Bob and Jill were determined to compensate for the suffering this child had undoubtedly experienced.

Their worries began at the airport. Juan seemed reluctant to make eye contact with his new parents. His easy smile seemed somehow forced. And their new son was extremely excited in the car on the way home. Bouncing from side to side, he was oblivious to requests—then demands—that he sit still. Juan was becoming a problem even on the first day with his new family.

By the time Juan was eight, Bob and Jill were asking the adoption agency to take him back. They couldn't handle him. He didn't appear to like them, much less love them. Juan acted as though they were supposed to give him anything he wanted and when he didn't get it, he exploded! This was not what they had expected from a poor kid rescued from a hopeless life in another country! Juan was violent both with his mother and with other children at school. The Christian school where he had been first enrolled suspended him permanently. Even the public school would not take him without a psychiatric evaluation.

The Luntons had a litany of complaints against their adopted child. Neighborhood children were afraid of him. Juan stole at will, even sneaking food and hiding it in his room despite an abundance in the house. When Bob and Jill asked why he took the food, Juan simply said that it was more "fun" that way. Finally, they had had enough.

Juan did not return to the Lunton home again.

A psychiatric evaluation determined that Juan was "sociopathic." He would need residential treatment and constant supervision for the foreseeable future. Bob and Jill were devastated! Not only had God prevented them from having children of their own, but He sent them a "monster" to adopt. What had they done, they wondered aloud, to deserve such unhappiness?

A month or two after my experiences with these two families, I received a frantic telephone call from June Wilson. She and her husband, Walt, were members of the adult Sunday School class Linda and I attended. They had heard me speak a few times when the regular teacher was on vacation or ill. Since my lessons usually related to family concerns, and especially regarding problems of Christian parenting, June called me seeking help.

We made an appointment for later that week. June and Walt arrived early for the appointment, eager to tell me about their eight-year-old son, Jamie. Always a difficult child, their first born was becoming much more difficult to control as he grew older—and bigger. These parents were reluctant to use physical discipline with their son. They'd relied exclusively on verbal responses and privilege removal to encourage good behavior and discipline bad behavior—but without much evidence of success.

Though June and Walt were extremely concerned about Jamie, it seemed theirs was a problem in parenting rather than that of a basic dysfunction in their son.

The most important clue was that Jamie was well-behaved in school and with his friends. As far as June and Walt could tell, their son was only a problem at home. Clearly, Jamie was choosing when and where to misbehave, indicating he was in control of his actions, bad as they were, when at home. Why June and Walt failed to realize this, I could not determine.

Second, there was no evidence of organic brain damage,

birth complications, or any other physical component that causes problem behavior in some children.

The third reason for suspecting a parenting problem was that Jamie behaved totally different when he was with me and his parents than when he was with his parents alone.

No, Jamie had pushed his limits at home and found them very, very loose. As most normal eight year olds would do, he was exploiting his parents' weakness to his advantage. What June and Walt—and especially Walt—needed help with was to toughen up the parent-child relationship, and mix in more firmness with the already abundant love.

I encouraged Walt to use physical means to force Jamie to behave if necessary, but to avoid hitting the child. I recommended the next time Jamie refused to pick up the toys in his room, Walt should pick *Jamie* up, take him to his room, close the door and stay there with him until the toys were picked up.

In the beginning, this took some persuasion on my part, but Walt eventually agreed. The quick and positive results we saw in Jamie were enough to convince the Wilsons that Jamie was okay and so were they.

What needed some slight change was some of the child-parent relationship patterns built up over the eight years of Jamie's life. Success breeds success, and Walt and June continued to be good parents for Jamie, and Jamie continued to respond to their love and strength.

Each of these three families were going through an experience with what I call "tough kids." They were searching for the mind of God, hoping to find some peace in their troubled family. They were asking the questions all of us ask when it happens in our family: "Why us, God?"

"Did we do something to deserve this?"

"Are you angry with us?"

13

"Are we such bad parents that we could have caused this to happen?"

"Is there any hope for our child?"

Let's consider for a moment the nature of children and parents, and the purpose of God in allowing us to become parents in the first place.

God's foreknowledge

Granted, it is no picnic raising a tough kid, but neither is that child an accident of nature or the punishment of God on sinful adults. The Psalmist wrote, "For you created my inmost being; you knit me together in my mother's womb. I praise you because I am fearfully and wonderfully made; your works are wonderful..." (Psalm 139:13-14).

And as God proclaimed to the prophet Jeremiah, "Before I formed you in the womb, I knew you..." (Jer.1:5).

So what's the point?

Simply this: God chooses us to meet the needs of our children, and not the reverse. Parents are selected to receive, on loan, children who are created by God and who need someone to raise them.

Let me explain this in a somewhat more personal way.

Our own story

Our first child, Laurie, was a "tough kid." Not as tough as Juan or Darrell, but much tougher than Jamie Wilson. In kindergarten, Laurie got into trouble for taking another child's watch. In first grade, she took someone's lunch money. Laurie told lies throughout her school years. She was a hyperactive child with an attention deficit disorder, and needed to be put on medication to help her sit still in school.

Laurie continued to have trouble in every school she attended. She did have some pretty good years—eventually graduating from a very strict Christian high school and becoming a registered nurse. But there was never a week of her growing up years when we were not worried about what she *might* be doing.

Sound a little paranoid? Actually, there's more to this than even these pages can communicate, but I ask you to trust me. We had reason to be concerned.

Linda and I have been to counselors, and many of them helped. But the greatest help came from a friend who shared about their own "tough kid."

With our friends' help, we learned that God prepares parents to receive the children He will create a little later. Linda and I had been on earth a combined total of 45 years, more or less, when we had Laurie, our first child.

Our *tough* child!

Forty-five years of education, of being parented by good parents, of going to church, being with friends, and falling in love with each other, of getting married and getting pregnant—this was our preparation.

Then God created this little girl we called Laurie.

As He formed this tiny human being, He knew that she would be hyperactive and have lots of problems growing up. But He deliberately selected us to be her parents. Did He say to Himself, "I'll give this little girl to the Millers because I know they can do the best for this child?" He knew we could deal with her.

And POP! There was Linda cradling Laurie in her loving arms, proudly showing her off to me and lots of relatives. We had been given our first child.

Did we know what difficulties Laurie would present? Of course not! Did God know? Absolutely! Did God select us carefully to be Laurie's parents? You had better believe it!

God selects specific people to be parents because He knows they can meet the needs of their children—even the tough ones! Sure, there are lots of people who fail—we live in a sinful world don't we?

People will mess themselves up with drugs and alcohol, make themselves crazy, and then abuse their children. They may even abandon their children to the care of others. And some parents will even kill their children. But every parent can be at least an adequate parent—if he or she chooses. So what is the lesson for parents like us who struggle with tough kids?

Simply this: God trusts those to whom He gives the greatest challenges

Tough kids and easy kids

Do you know a "perfect" family somewhere? Maybe in church? You know, the family where the children are almost never bad, and mom and dad just seem so happy in their parenting? People like that are enough to make you dizzy sometimes, aren't they?

Well, there's two possible explanations for those near-perfect children. The first is that those folks are really terrific parents, and they have done a wonderful job of raising their children. (I am not being sarcastic here. Of course there are many, many outstanding parents, and this is a real possibility.)

But it is also possible that this couple with the well-behaved kids are just average parents. God, knowing they would be just average, gave them *easy children* to raise!

Did you get that? *Easy children!*

God, knowing they would be just average parents, gave

them easy, rather than tough, kids to raise! Are you feeling better yet? Now consider the families with tough kids—the one's like our oldest, who was always in trouble.

Two possibilities exist as well for parents with tough kids. One, and I can imagine you have figured out where I am going with this, is that this couple are not very good parents, and ineffective parenting is showing up in disobedient, unruly, destructive, mean-spirited, and generally obnoxious, kids.

Bad parents equals bad kids. Okay—that is one definite possibility.

But it is also possible that those parents with the tough kid are really outstanding parents. It could be that God has entrusted a difficult child to them for care and upbringing! Feeling better yet?

I don't know about you, but this insight from another "challenged parent" really helped me put things in perspective when we were trying to parent Laurie. And what it means to me today is that being "handed" a Down-Syndrome child to raise is not a curse from an angry God. Instead, it's a compliment to your ability to raise such a child.

The normal question, of course, is why God creates difficult kids in the first place. Well, that is *way* beyond my ability to understand, I'll admit. God doesn't tell us the answer, but He does give us a warning. It is in Matthew 18:7—"Woe to the world because of the things that cause people to sin! Such things must come, but woe to the man through whom they come!"

I take this verse to mean that God knows that in a sinful world children will suffer. Some will be born with handicaps and limitations; others will die in accidents or be crippled because of another's negligence. Still others will be beaten, abused, and neglected by adults—even their parents. God is telling us that He knows this will happen because the world is steeped in sin. But He also declares, "You had better not be the person who offends one of my little ones!"

Being human, we can only tremble at the significance of such a warning.

Down-syndrome babies are born into the world because there is sin in the world. Non-compliant boys and girls populate our families because there is sin in the world. Hyperactive, learning-disabled, psychotic, sociopathic, and self-destructive children live in this world because there is sin in the world.

But you and I had better not be that one who becomes a tool of sin and injures children in some way. It is our task to do our best with the less-than-perfect children God delivers into our less-than-perfect hands for a few years of child-rearing

Facing reality

One of the main messages of this book is that Christian parents need to face up to reality and deal with the problems in their families as they arise. I am a licensed professional counselor in Virginia and I carry a client load of about ten families at a time. I say this only to support my contention that too many parents like us wait too long to get their children the help they need. I've seen it happen over and over.

We don't want to admit to problems in our family. We believe people will think we are failures as parents—that we will be embarrassed when we go to church. We're afraid that someone will find out and gossip about us. We don't want others to think we haven't tried *everything* to help our children.

And so problems fester and become worse.

Moms and dads argue more because of the stress of raising a tough kid. Siblings suffer too. They get less attention because their parents are always worrying about the problem child. Their good behavior goes ignored while the bad behavior of the other kid gets all their parents' attention. So they begin to resent this brother or sister who is "bad." Before long, the family has become the patient along with the difficult child.

But this kind of thing doesn't have to happen.

If only mom and dad had swallowed their pride and gotten help when it could have done the most good—right away, as soon as they began telling themselves that they have a problem child on their hands!

Finding "Normal"

Turn your imagination loose for a moment. Travel along with Mr. and Mrs. Everyone, who were looking for that mythical "normal" child they assumed to exist somewhere. "Normal," when found, would allow them to set the behavior standard by which they could evaluate all kids.

"What a blessing that would be," thought Mr. and Mrs. Everyone, "if only we could be the ones to discover Normal. Maybe he or she is living in some remote village in the Yucatan. Or on a farm in Iowa. Perhaps Normal even lives in Russia, or in a European city—but Normal *must* be alive somewhere.

Despite their best efforts, however, the Everyones failed in their attempt to locate Normal. Finally realizing their predicament, they decided to use the next best alternative—children in their own area. So they went into the schools and neighborhoods observing other children. Sure enough, they found many, many "Near Normals" who allowed them to evaluate their child's behavior. And the Everyones lived happily ever after. Until adolescence, that is, when they had to start all over again!

Somewhere out there may be a "normal" kid, but you couldn't prove it by me. I sure haven't seen a kid I'd be willing to use as an example of "normal." It just seems that children of all ages are so different that getting a grasp on what is normal is just about impossible.

Yet finding "normal" is still the challenge for all parents. Even those with children or teens who haven't been major problems (and probably will not become problems later on).

It isn't that well-behaved, polite and respectful children are abnormal or bad. But there can be bad reasons for their being polite and well-behaved. Fear of being beaten, for example, will motivate most children to behave themselves whether they really want to or not.

The point is simply this: all parents should make a reasonable attempt to evaluate, by comparison, the needs of and the behavioral standards for their own children. The kids need not be told what is going on, nor informed of results. But it is generally agreed that one major responsibility of good parents everywhere is to determine the needs of their children, and to do their best to meet those needs. And needs cannot be determined in isolation; human children are just too diverse. No, to do an adequate job, it takes parental insight and intuition and knowledge of what most other kids in the same age group are like.

Parenting isn't forever

Being a charter member of NAPSCM (The National Association for the Prevention of the Spread of Country

Music), I'm not up on the latest in country music. But one old-time, semi-gospel country song asks, "Will the circle be unbroken, in the sweet bye and bye...?"

But there is no heavenly "family circle" in Scripture. That's just a sweet and sentimental notion.

The Bible indicates that in heaven, we will be as close to people we've never met as we will be to our own family members. While the idea of staying together as family units throughout eternity is understandable, it's just an expression of our humanity—and our inability to fully understand what heaven is going to be like for believers.

The Bible stresses over and over again the practicality and functionality of the family unit on earth. The reason for families is the raising of children. This is what God ordained in making two sexes (instead of five or six), and in determining that children will be born to their biological parents. And they eventually grow into adults. This may come as no surprise, but the happy lesson for parents of tough kids is that as far as parenting goes, "this too shall pass." We will not be parents forever. And we will not be dealing with these crises for the rest of our lives.

There is a blue horizon—a horizon of cure and recovery for the disturbed child God has placed in your care. Or it may be a horizon made blue and sunny by the passage of time and the growth to adulthood of that tough kid. The problem is that too many tough-kid problems seem to be unsolvable by anything except the passing of years.

Problems awaiting a solution

But there are answers. God placed these kids in our care because He knows us and trusts us to meet the child's needs appropriately.

The human sin nature being what it is, all our children are tough kids to some degree. This is true in the same way that all our families are dysfunctional to a greater or lesser extent.

I don't want to minimize the pain and sense of failure common to parents of tough kids.

I do want to acknowledge that it is normal to feel this way when things go badly. But it is also normal to seek solutions and expect they will be found. God didn't give us these children expecting us to fail. (Just remember, what you or I may consider a failure with a child, God—knowing what is really inside that child—may consider a success!)

Did that make sense to you?

Let me put it this way. A parent may evaluate a given action with his or her tough kid as a failure. But God may see their action as a success—*in that it's the best we can expect at this moment with this particular child.*

The crucial challenge for all mature Christians is to think with the mind of Christ—and that is never more true than when working with tough kids. In fact, to survive, we need to become biblically "tough parents."

What makes a "Tough Parent"?

"Tough Parents" are committed to 10 important beliefs:

1. *We are not the creators nor the owners of this child.*

He or she belongs to God first, and to us second. God is more responsible for this child than we are. So if there is an inborn condition in this child that is becoming a problem, we are not at fault for that condition. We will simply do our best.

2. *We admit that we have a problem child.*

We will fight our embarrassment and sense of failure and do what is best for this child no matter what our friends, family, or pastor thinks. We will do what we believe is best for this child and we will determine this through prayer, study, and good counsel.

3. *We acknowledge that this child's disobedience and rebellion are a function of his or her human nature.*

We will discipline and not punish. We will be motivated by compassion instead of revenge. And we will persist in our loving discipline even if the stars fall. We will stay in charge of this child as long as we are able.

4. *We will be optimistic.*

God didn't entrust this child to our care to drive us crazy or to make the child worse. There is an answer awaiting discovery. We will be the discoverers.

5. *We have the right to require our child to act responsibly.*

We do not have to apologize for doing right, even if it makes our child unhappy.

6. *We will not be fooled, manipulated, embarrassed, or intimidated by our child's behavior.*

7. *We will assure that our child experiences the natural consequences of both good and bad behavior.*

We will be careful to recognize and reinforce appropriate behavior, and equally careful to deal with inappropriate behavior.

8. *We will confront the problems placed before us.*

We will not deny their existence nor attempt to beat them into submission. We will respond as our child requires us to respond. The agenda is his.

9. *We will maintain our marital relationship and love for each other no matter what our child does.*

We will not allow our marriage to be threatened by this child. We will maintain our ministry and our testimony before the Lord and His people, even in the darkest days.

10. *We will not surrender to our child, and we will not surrender our child to the world.* We will not quit!

Darrell, Juan and Jamie

Several years have passed since the incidents I mentioned at the beginning of this chapter.

We know what became of Jamie. His improvement has continued to this day and he shows no indication of getting worse. Both the Kravchuks and Luntons remain in the area, and I have kept up with developments through mutual friends and personal conversations. Here is what has happened:

Darrell, the young "cat-killer," spent nearly a year in a residential facility for emotionally-disturbed children. Darrell has recovered to about 80 percent of what his parents consider to be his potential.

He is now a young adolescent, really a "pre-teen." Darrell is required to have weekly group counseling sessions at the local mental health center, an experience he now seems to enjoy and look forward to. The therapist is very skilled at building relationships with kids such as Darrell.

Darrell is not allowed to be alone with small children yet. He retains some element of explosiveness, but is clearly working hard to keep himself under control. It is obvious that he now wants to stay out of trouble. As far as anyone can tell, he has not set any more fires, nor hurt any more small children or pets.

We do not know why Darrell had such a problem in the first place. We often suspect some type of abuse or organic brain problems in children like Darrell, but none were detected. His premature birth was difficult and traumatic, requiring him to be in the hospital for the first two months of his life. So it is possible that there was a failure to bond at that time. But we aren't sure.

Darrell seems to be okay now, though. His parents acted quickly and decisively once they knew what was happening.

And the child psychiatrist who worked with Darrell said that was a key to his recovery. We'll have to wait and see what the future holds for Darrell, but we are optimistic at the moment.

But then there's Juan.

Sadly, Juan's story is a little more typical of older kids who exhibit poor impulse control. All we have been allowed to know about him is that Juan was placed in several foster homes between age eight when the Luntons gave him up and age fourteen when he ran away. Juan told some of his friends at school that he was going to run away to California, and the authorities believe this is what happened. One of his foster parents received a phone call the Christmas when Juan would have been fifteen, but he wouldn't tell them where he was. He has not been heard from since. Juan would be about eighteen now, but no one is optimistic about his chances of survival on the street.

These are only three true cases among many that will follow in the pages to come. Darrell, Juan, and Jamie gave us about a two/thirds success rate, but the real picture for troubled kids is much less optimistic.

What will make the difference for my kids and yours is what we learn as parents and what we can bring ourselves to do for them. Tough kids are no picnic. They are as unhappy with themselves as others are with them. But if there is a caring family behind a kid—any kid—he or she has a multiplied opportunity for improvement compared to kids without a family for support.

I just want to encourage you when it comes to dealing with tough kids. We *can* do it.

We would not have been assigned these kids to raise unless God knew we could do what is necessary. The following chapters explain the problems and offer suggestions as to how to correct them. Correction is possible. Linda and I are not only survivors of a tough kid, but victorious overcomers as well.

You, too, can overcome!

Semi-Tough Kids

The ability to parent effectively is not limited by the kinds of problems our children bring with them into the world. Some parents will have an easier time of child-rearing than others for no apparent reason. And many will find parenting more difficult for equally mysterious reasons. The children delivered into our care by an all-wise God need what we can do for them. And because they are human too, they may be limited in what can be done with their lives.

The destiny of children is not solely up to parents.

Parents who are charged with the responsibility for caring for a chronically ill, Down-syndrome, or cerebral-palsied child are in exactly the same category as parents who raise a hyperactive, learning disabled, or emotionally disturbed child. The nature of the challenge we face in our parenting reflects the trust God places in us who care for his children. It is not a reflection of an inherited sin or God's desire to get even with us for past misbehavior. God would never require a child to be sacrificed to mental retardation or deafness to atone for the sins of parents.

Challenging children are a compliment from God!

Yes, I know it was quite a while before the parents of the children we met in the first chapter came to believe this, but God's truth is not limited by our ability to understand it. Whether your children are like Darrell, Juan, Jamie, or any of the number of children and teens we will be meeting later, the challenge and level of responsibility are the same: Do your best. Trust God. God loves the "good enough" parent!

The semi-tough kid

We read about the tough and super-tough kids and wonder how parents can live that way. We learn of terrible things happening in homes all over America, and are frightened that these things may occur in our homes some day. For most parents though, kids like Darrell or Juan will not become part of their experience. Yes, it could happen, and we will look at "super-tough" kids later on. But for the most part, the problems we face with our kids will fall into the "semi-tough" category.

A semi-tough kid is hard to control and difficult to discipline. He's an "I-can't-figure-out-why-he-won't-behave" type kid who drives parents crazy. But he doesn't frighten them the way Darrell and Juan frightened their parents. A semi-tough kid is a three year old who absolutely will not leave the family breakables on the shelf, no matter how hard or often he or she is spanked, scolded, or made to stand in the corner.

The semi-tough kid is a seven year old who will not do his homework or stay in his seat and who, with the proper opportunity, will make embarrassing noises each time the teacher passes his seat. And the semi-tough kid is a fourteen year old with a razor-blade earring who will tolerate being grounded for life for the chance to listen to "Tortured Cousin," "Squashed Spaniel," or some other heavy metal rock and roll group.

In other words, semi-tough kids are kids who behave the way many of *us* did when we were their age. Only now we are the parents instead of the kid. Isn't it amazing how hard we try to keep our children from learning about *our* childish or teen activities? We act as if they really believe we were the perfect youngsters we want them to be (and our parents wanted us to be).

Parental amnesia

The burden our kids bear is having parents who have forgotten what it was like to be a kid. This form of forgetting, called "parental amnesia," is epidemic in the general population of parents. It's even more widespread among Christian parents, who probably feel a little more guilty and embarrassed than others.

So when it comes time to make the difficult decisions in the grey areas of family life and parenting, Christian parents tend to forget what we did when we dated or hung out at the mall or on the corner. We try very hard to forget what *we* did back in the ice age (or so it seems to our teenagers), and we will usually rationalize our activities should they become known by saying "Well, don't forget, things were different in those days."

Take a few minutes some day and talk over with your husband or wife what you would be willing to share with your kids that would help them feel more human when they mess up. What can you remember about your parents' discipline that might help in the present situation? And very important is your responsibility not to overreact to a behavior that is usually no more serious than it was when we did the same thing a couple decades ago.

Sure, the world is a more dangerous place than it was when we were young. This is obviously true no matter what your age. But Christian parents don't have to make problems worse by exaggerating their importance out of all proportion to the true seriousness of the misbehavior.

Let's examine child and adolescent misbehavior that would fall into the semi-tough category. This is where most of our kids will be correctly categorized when the day comes that brings the telephone call from the school, police department, or neighbor.

Why kids misbehave

Suzanne was a normal five year old in every way but one. She was a highly skilled tantrum artist. Somehow little Suzanne learned that she deserved to have what she wanted, and she deserved to have it now. And woe be unto that person who did not move fast enough, or who got in her way when she was on the move. Her parents described this bright five year old as "unstoppable" when it came to getting what she wanted. Her ultimate weapon was a screaming, heel-banging, purple-faced tantrum.

I witnessed one of Suzanne's tantrums in our waiting room one day and I must admit, it was a masterpiece of manipulation. I don't know what it was that she wanted, but she either didn't get it quickly enough or it may not have been available at all. But there was no question who was in charge of that waiting room for those few minutes.

Mom and dad were embarrassed, and the other people in the waiting room did their best to hide behind their magazines. I was shocked at such explosiveness and pure volume coming out of such a small body, but there was no escape from Suzanne when she was into a full-blown tantrum At only five years of age, Suzanne had perfected her tantrum skills.

Each move was carefully planned. Suzanne's parents told me that she would not throw herself to the floor for her tantrum, but would lie down carefully so she wouldn't be hurt. She'd check first to make sure the right people were present in the room or within hearing—and away she'd go. I had the feeling that Suzanne even carefully computed the possible return on her investment of energy in the tantrum. Her mother said that Suzanne rarely threw a tantrum until dad was rested upon his return from work, and never before dinner.

Suzanne, at five years of age, already knew not to get dad angry when he was also tired, for to do so was to risk an actual spanking. And it was unwise, Suzanne knew, to risk being sent to your room *before* dinner.

And then there was Robert. Always "Robert," never "Bobby," as I was informed on our first visit. Robert was thirteen years old and just beginning to experiment with being independent. He had a lot to learn! So did Robert's parents.

Robert was the oldest of three children and the only boy. Robert's parents speculated that his only-son and only-grandson status probably contributed to his being "spoiled." There wasn't much doubt in my mind that this was an important factor—though I knew that in counseling teenagers and parents, the presenting problem (in this case rebellion), is often not the true problem.

As I listened to Robert's parents talk about their son, the depth of their concern was obvious. The family were professing Christians, weekly church attenders, and tithed regularly. They stated that there was no deep, secret sin guarded in the family. In fact, they really seemed to be what they claimed to be. As was true of the other children, Robert was raised in the church. He had made a profession of faith at age eight and was baptized a few months later.

To listen to Robert's parents, there was no warning of what they were seeing in their son today. Virtually overnight, they said, Robert had changed from a "pretty good kid" to a behavior problem. Robert would not do anything without grumbling and complaining.

"Take out the trash!" mom would command!

"Grumble, grumble, grumble," they would hear as Robert carried the trash container outside.

"Would you clean up your room?" dad would ask.

"Soon as I get a chance," their son would reply.

"Is your homework done yet?" mom would question.

"Yes, mom. Don't worry about it," Robert would answer.

It didn't seem to matter what his parents requested, absolutely nothing was done without complaining. Oh, Robert almost always eventually did what he was told, but his parents were concerned about his apparent lack of respect and his lack of willingness to help without complaining.

Both Suzanne and Robert were suffering the same affliction, though in different forms. Both children had experienced a degree of ineffective parenting that had unwittingly contributed to the misbehavior their parents were now concerned about. We can use these two cases to help us analyze "semi-tough" kids and find ways to deal with their behaviors and attitudes.

Principles of youth misbehavior—*or, why they do it and how we can stop it!*

1. Why unacceptable behavior happens: *Behavior is learned through a series of interactions between children and their world.*

Suzanne and Robert entered this world devoid of methodology for misbehavior. The Bible tells us that we are born in sin and tend to misbehave under any circumstances.

Each child, however, must learn *how* to misbehave.

Suzanne threw tantrums because she had learned along the way that this method was effective in getting what she wanted.

Robert misbehaved because he had discovered that he could grumble and complain up to a certain level before having the wrath of dad come down on his head. Robert grumbled because he was a human thirteen-year-old male and this is what they do—*if we let them!*

Suzanne threw tantrums because she had learned that tantrums produce results, and because she was a human female who had learned in her first five years how to manipulate mom and dad.

For both Robert and Suzanne, the single significant issue of their misbehavior was power and control.

This is a nearly universal truth for semi-tough kids. Their parents were trying to teach them that they must behave but failed somehow to get that message across. Robert and Suzanne learned by doing, and they did what helped them gain a feeling of independence, power, and control over self and situation. When their parents failed to enforce their commands, the children realized that they did not mean it in the first place, and unacceptable behavior resulted.

What to do about it: *Re-teach!*

Suzanne and Robert must experience a new set of circumstances that will "un-teach" the dysfunctional lessons they'd learned and "re-teach" better lessons. Their parents must restructure their environment so that their children learn that old methods (tantrums, grumbling) no longer work.

Some new behaviors (obedience, cooperativeness) will work, however, to get them what they want. So when Suzanne learns that the tantrum is now going to be ignored, and *she will be disciplined* by being sent to her room, this five year old will quickly learn to get her needs met by asking politely for what she wants and being able to wait to have her requests (not demands) granted.

Robert will experience a new set of circumstances in the family. He will learn that mom and dad have begun asking his opinion on things, granting reasonable requests without argument and generally treating this thirteen year old as a young adult rather than an old child. When Robert feels power in doing right, doing wrong will lose most of it's attraction.

2. Why unacceptable behavior happens: *Children learn most effectively by watching.*

Everything people do has first been imagined or actually seen in others. Suzanne was an only child. She could not have learned her tantrum routine from brothers or sisters (as is the case in most families). But I suggested to her mom that she try to find out if any of Suzanne's playmates also threw tantrums. Sure enough, Suzanne had not one but *two* playmates who regularly used tantrums to get their way at home.

Simply put, Suzanne saw what worked at a friend's house and decided to try it for herself. And guess what? It had worked! So should we be surprised that Suzanne throws tantrums? Of course not. Suzanne is a human child with a fully functioning brain, and she is naturally able to learn from what works.

Basically the same process happened with Robert. He had witnessed his *father* grumbling about household chores. He also saw that mom asked less often if there were complaints and delays. Mom would often just give up and do it herself rather than wait for husband or son to do as she had asked. And Robert was a normally lazy, unmotivated thirteen year old who would get out of work if he could.

He simply learned by watching his father—and then behaved like him.

What to do about it: Re-model.

Suzanne could no longer play in the homes of her two friends who threw tantrums to get their way. She could play with other children of course. And she could resume playing with her manipulative friends once her own tantrums had stopped. Suzanne had to be removed from the presence of the dysfunctional models (the two playmates and their weak parents), and encouraged to be with children and parents who did not use tantrums.

Robert, on the other hand, would be left alone on this point. The focus would be on his father, the other grumbler. Once Robert's dad understood the process by which his son had learned to complain, he was willing to work harder to set a better example for him. This delighted his wife, who could look forward to better behavior in both son and husband as a result.

3. Why unacceptable behavior happens: Good and bad behavior quickly rewarded will each occur more often in the future.

Humans have powerful brains, and it doesn't take very long for most of us to figure out what works. We learn that to reach for that big white thing (the oven, for example) in the place where we eat (the kitchen) makes the big lady who feeds me (mom) slap the little thing at the end of my arm (my hand).

Robert learned early in life that dad's grumbling sometimes got him out of doing what he didn't want to do. Respecting his dad, it was normal for Robert to imitate his behavior. When the grumbling proved to work for him too, Robert figured he was on to something—which of course, he was!

But when he learned that the complaining and grumbling only worked to get him into more work, the behavior stopped. When Robert saw the smile on mom's face when he obeyed without complaining, he felt even better about cooperating.

Suzanne too, faced a new set of circumstances at home. Her parents learned to quickly remove her from the family at the first sign of tantrum behavior. They learned that tantrums are thrown to gain power and attention, so they placed her in her room and ignored her for a few minutes. Suzanne could return to the family only when she was finished with her rampage. When she began to rebel less and make normal requests for what she wanted, she quickly learned that better results were forthcoming.

What to do about it: *Change the reward structure.*

Both of the children, different as they were, easily learned to avoid punishments and to seek rewards. All that had to happen was that their parents needed to learn a better way of structuring their family so these things could happen. As Robert's father said to me during one session, "This isn't rocket science, but it sure works!"

4. Why unacceptable behavior happens: *Parents pay attention to the wrong behaviors .*

Both the parents of Robert and of Suzanne were encouraged to add one missing element to their attempts at child control and correction. I suggested that they consider ignoring the unwanted behavior at times. Instead, they needed to notice when the behavior was not occurring and pay attention to that. This process is called *"catch them being good,"* and is well known to school teachers who are effective disciplinarians in their classrooms.

What to do about it: Ignore the bad and notice the good.

In the case of Suzanne, the tantrums usually did not bring on a forced placement in her room. Instead, mom and dad just got up and left the room when the tantrum started. This was effective for two reasons.

First, tantrums are *always* done for attention.

So when the audience leaves, there is no longer a reason to continue. Suzanne was learning that instead of getting attention (which could lead to her wishes being fulfilled), mom and dad were leaving the room and depriving her of both her audience (attention) and the people who could give her what she wanted. Tantrums became a "lose-lose" proposition for this five year old, and she caught on very quickly.

For a thirteen year old like Robert, it was a little more complicated. If his parents left him alone, it would mean he could avoid doing what they wanted, and this was not acceptable to them.

What Robert's parents learned to do was to "catch him being good" and quickly praise and reward him for doing right.

When Robert was asked to carry the trash out back and did so while forgetting to grumble, his parents made a big deal of how grown up he was becoming, and not complaining "like a little kid would do."

37

Praise like this is very important to the self-concept of all teens and children. Although it may be apparently ignored by "cool" teens, such praise still makes a great deal of difference. Robert's parents combined their ignoring of the unwanted behavior with attention and praise for wanted behavior and saw a positive change in their son.

5. Why unacceptable behavior happens: *Parents reward when they think they are punishing.*

Suzanne had resorted to tantrum behavior because she found it worked to meet her needs. Without knowing it, Suzanne conducted a serious, if accidental, scientific experiment related to getting what she wanted or needed. She saw her friends throw tantrums and observed the results.

Then she tried it with *her* parents, and experienced the same results. And a behavior pattern was born!

Even though her parents sometimes spanked her, and even though she did not like the spanking, for Suzanne, a spanking or scolding was better than being ignored, chased away, or refused. What her parents learned was that in young children especially, trading a scolding, spanking, or isolation for attention is standard practice.

For young children, the choice between feeling ignored and left out or being paid attention to through being disciplined for unacceptable behavior is an easy choice.

With Robert, the process was roughly the same. He needed to feel more grown up than he was allowed to feel at the time. This necessitated an alternate strategy for him to feel grown up. He knew that rebellion and misbehavior are signs that adolescence has arrived, and chose that method to feel more like a teenager. His grumbling and complaining brought negative messages and punishment his way. But they were better in this thirteen-year-old's mind than feeling like a little kid—even a well behaved little kid.

Robert's parents thought they were discouraging his rebellion, mild though it was. In fact, they were playing right into his hands. Robert told me on one occasion, "The more they holler at me, the older and more grown up I feel."

Robert's parents were rewarding bad behavior but thought they were discouraging it. They couldn't understand why such behavior continued.

What to do about it: The parents of both these children needed to re-evaluate their discipline techniques.

Each found the element of their discipline that had opposite effects to what they expected.

Suzanne was helped when her parents began to combine walking away from her tantrums with paying attention to her before she needed to create a scene to feel noticed.

Suzanne would still be spanked and otherwise physically controlled when this more planned approach could not be implemented. But within three months of her parents' changing their methods, Suzanne's tantrums were a thing of the past.

Robert, being several years older than Suzanne, presented a different kind of challenge. His parents also needed to try and ignore his under-the-breath grumblings but at the same time, catch him being good *and* reward him with extra privileges for acting so "grown-up."

Robert's motivation for misbehaving seemed to be a desire to be treated more like a teenager than a child. When his parents began to do so, Robert's behavior improved.

In both cases, parents had been rewarding bad behavior instead of discouraging it, and each was unaware that it was happening.

6. Why unacceptable behavior happens: *Parents deal with only one controlling factor and ignore the other.*

To discipline semi-tough kids effectively, parents must consider both antecedent and consequent events. What happens just before the incident of bad behavior? What happens immediately after the behavior?

These are equally important factors in discipline.

If discipline is to work in helping children behave more appropriately, parents must be able to figure out what was going on just prior to the outburst and what happened just afterward.

What to do about it: *Analyze the process!*

Suzanne's parents caught on quickly to the idea of ignoring her unacceptable behavior, but it took a while longer before they were ready to start thinking about what led up to the tantrums. They needed to discover and analyze the chain of events that occurred prior to Suzanne's "going nuclear." How was she feeling? Did the tantrums occur mostly in the morning, afternoon, or evening? Who was present in the room when the tantrum began? Just mom? Just dad? Both? Did the tantrums happen only following a refusal of some sort, or did they happen without any predictability?

Robert's parents also needed to consider preceding as well as following events. Did his grumbling happen more on school days or weekends? Was Robert worse after having spent time with certain friends? Was he better behaved with mom or dad? Were there times when Robert did not grumble and complain? What was different about those times?

There are so many questions for parents to consider, but each of us must become good tacticians and strategists in our parenting. And this is never more apparent than when trying to understand pre- and post-misbehavior in a family setting.

The reason God assigned these children to us was because He knows we are capable of doing what is required. So we want to be very careful that we don't give up and surrender our kids to the world simply because they are becoming a challenge.

Jesus reminded us to "See that you do not look down on one of these little ones. For I tell you that their angels in heaven always see the face of my Father in heaven." (Mat.18:10)

We must not surrender these children to their human desires and emotions. To give up on a youngster is to "look down on" them, to not care anymore for them, to put *our* needs above theirs. We have no choice. We must continue to fight *for* them, even if it means battling *with* them for control.

Tough Kids

God loves the challenged parent as much as he loves the challenging child. But when the Robbins family talked about their relationships, it was apparent that none were feeling much love right then. There was so much turmoil at home that it seemed that they and their son hardly liked each other anymore, much less loved one another.

Carter

Carter Robbins was fifteen going on twenty, to use his parents' description, and he was in no mood to wait very long to be grown up.

Carter's early years were not very distinctive. His birth was normal and he was the middle child in a family of two older brothers and two younger sisters. Everyone agreed that he had an unremarkable elementary school experience, but Carter slowly began getting into mild trouble in the seventh grade. First there were calls from his school about cutting classes and lying to cover up. Then, in the eighth grade, Carter's parents learned he had begun to use tobacco when he was with his friends.

At home, Carter bullied his younger sisters and taunted his older brothers. They would not take much hassling from him, and didn't hesitate to deal with him physically. Strange as it may seem, Carter seemed to almost welcome these losing battles.

His behavior with his parents had deteriorated to the point where they truly thought their son did not love them, much less his siblings.

Carter's ninth-grade year began with a distinctive "thud" when he was suspended from school the first week of classes for cursing at a teacher in the lunch room. Three days at home only seemed to make him even more angry, and when his parents would not change their mind about his being grounded, he ran away.

Gone for three days at age fourteen, Carter Robbins had crossed the line from more or less "normal" teenage rebellion to a level of behavior meriting serious professional and parental attention.

It was later discovered that this fourteen year old had stayed with a high school drop-out "friend" and his girl friend across town.

When the juvenile authorities brought Carter home, they talked privately with his parents. The authorities warned the Robbinses that their son's new friends were known drug users and were strongly suspected of dealing drugs as well.

By the time Carter returned home, he had gotten a "radical" haircut that was totally out of line with his previous friends and unacceptable to the family. The next day, his mother noticed that he had also had his left ear pierced, though no earring had been seen yet. It was in this situation that Carter Robbins entered his fifteenth year. It was going to get worse before it got better!

Shauna

I met Shauna Houston and her parents at a transition conference in the adolescent unit of a local psychiatric hospital. Mr. and Mrs. Houston had placed their thirteen-year-old daughter there for a psychiatric evaluation following a suicide attempt.

The attempt followed a family blowup over Shauna's demand that she be allowed to date a much older (and far from acceptable) young man. Her parents were convinced that they were correct in not wanting to see their daughter dating *anyone* at her age, much less someone several years older.

Shauna had returned home after ten days of therapy and evaluation, but she was unchanged in her determination to do as she pleased. Once home, she announced that unless she was allowed to date anyone she wished, to be treated as the adult she believed herself to be, she would run away. And if her parents continued to force her to return home, she would kill herself or get pregnant, whichever she felt more like at the time.

Shauna wasn't pulling any punches, and her parents were frantic to find an answer. The answer was going to be more difficult than they ever imagined.

Allen

Allen Combes is the youngest of this trio of tough kids. He was only six years old when his parents acknowledged they had a problem child. Allen's parents had separated and then divorced within the previous two years; Allen had not lived with his dad in the home since he turned four.

For a four year old, Allen had vivid memories of his parents arguing and fighting. He could describe in detail the climactic event—the night his father came home to "make up" and wound up in jail for beating up Allen's mother on the front lawn. Allen had been severely traumatized by this single event. Since that night, he had not experienced one day without intense anger.

This boy was angry at everyone. But without being able to understand or explain it, he seemed to target himself for the greatest blame—and the greatest abuse.

Recently, Allen had been picking more and more fights at school. Just weeks before I met the family, he had struck his mother with his fist. This six year old was fast becoming a case for self-destruction, and we needed to intervene right away. A lot of secrets would be revealed and confessions made, and after intense counseling, Allen would slowly get better.

But there's one thing about these three families I haven't mentioned yet. They are all professing Christians.

This is true for nearly all the families discussed in this book. In each family, parents and children, even Allen, have confessed Jesus Christ as personal Lord and Savior. They were Christians all, yet all were in deep trouble.

This will not surprise those experienced in dealing with Christian families. For years, pastors have warned that the problems of the world were invading the Christian church and families. Those warnings have proven abundantly true.

While Christianity is a part of the story in most, but not all, of the families in this book, true Christianity can become the answer for any family facing the kind of tough, challenging kids we are examining.

Our job in these first chapters is to learn something of the ways of difficult children. What is it that troubles Carter,

Shauna, and Allen? How can we measure the level of trouble they are in? And finally, what can we do about it?

For right now, let's see if we can fit these three tough kids into the appropriate category so they can be understood.

Categories of Tough Kids

It is always difficult to classify children and adolescents who are still growing and changing. The American Psychiatric Association does not allow adult labels to be placed on those under eighteen specifically because of the changes still to take place in many of these young people.

It is also important to acknowledge that labels and categories do not allow for much cross-over or combining. And we must also take into account the unique dynamics of each family as they deal with a difficult child or teenager.

Finally, Christian parents must recognize that these labels, categories, and classifications are reflections of human imperfections, including imperfections in those doing the classifying.

Only God knows with certainty what is really troubling any tough kid.

So we must be always in an attitude of prayer and humility, asking God's guidance in knowing what best to do for the children and teens in our care.

Aggressive tough kids

The aggressive tough kid is one who is willing, even eager to push to get what he or she wants.

This tough kid gets angry at the drop of a hat, has an explosive temper, is easily frustrated. Furthermore, he is quick to blame others for the frustration he experiences, and appears openly hostile to authority figures. Carter Robbins showed some traits of the aggressive kid, but he fits better into another category to be looked at in a moment.

The aggressive tough kid can be frightening to parents and other adults, and even to peers. What seems to be most intimidating is the constant attitude of anger and hostility that seems ready to be aimed at anyone who frustrates his or her wishes.

Dealing with the aggressive kid

This kid often must be removed from the family for a time. That way, the young person can get the therapy most needed in determining what is really upsetting him or her. This treatment is difficult or impossible, depending on the seriousness of the behavior, in an uncontrolled environment such as a home where people who may be contributing to the problem still live.

Note that I did not say that the home was the problem, or that the family members were at fault.

Rather, the home and family may be inadvertently *contributing* to the problem behavior, even while being a pretty good home, with pretty good—or even excellent—parents. Again, the determining issue here is the seriousness of the problem behavior, and we will examine that process at the end of this chapter

Passive tough kids

The passive tough kid is more likely to be female and to live in a strict home. This tough kid, as is true of all these categories, can be found in Christian families.

But, the passive tough kid is *more likely* to be found in a Christian home because of the prevalence of over-control and over-discipline in the conservative wing of modern Christianity.

Passive tough kids will act out by sabotaging family plans, such as getting "sick" at the last minute, or by spilling something on their clothing as the family is leaving to go to an important family event that the tough kid didn't want to attend. Passive tough kids will whine and complain to try and get their way. And when they fail, they will withdraw and simply refuse to cooperate.

The passive kid will tell stories to the younger children to get them upset so that they in turn will get mom and dad upset. This will be a form of revenge for some refusal or frustration of something that the child or teenager wanted.

Dealing with the passive tough kid

These children or teens need to experience failure in manipulating parents. They need to learn that what they are doing not only fails to get them what they want, but also gets them disciplined in some way.

Disciplining the passive youngster can be especially difficult because they often seem to be *partially* obedient. Parents need to recognize this incomplete obedience as just another way of trying to gain control of the family without getting into major trouble. The passive child is often the coward among tough kids, but while the fear may be greater, the motivation to be in control of the family is the same.

Cultural conformist tough kid

The tough kid in this category identifies with a group outside the family and church, and with kids outside the former group of friends, as well.

The cultural conformist has taken on a new family, a new

reference group, a new identity. This tough kid is acting out and misbehaving because he wants to be like the other kids, the ones who have impressed him with how tough and radical they are.

Carter Robbins fits this category in many ways. Carter clearly had adopted another group of young people as his friends. His behavior when with his family indicated that he was becoming anesthetized to their values and beliefs, and was intent on convincing them and others that he no longer cared what they thought about anything.

Carter was showing everyone just how "peer oriented" he was—and that there was no chance of persuading him to do anything he didn't want to do.

Dealing with the cultural conformist

Because Carter was only fifteen when all this took place, his parents had some options that would not be available if their son had been a few years older. Carter wound up misbehaving in even worse ways than I have shared with you, and his parents decided to try and place their son in a Christian boarding school for difficult teenagers.

Carter was not aware of this until they literally arrived at the gate of the school. His dad had asked two of Carter's uncles to "go on a fishing trip" with him and his son. Unfortunately, this was deceptive. Yet his father truly feared that Carter would run away, or even try to hurt himself if he knew in advance what was to happen. After driving most of the night to their "fishing" destination with Carter asleep in the back seat, they pulled onto the grounds of the boarding school.

Of course Carter was livid with anger, but he was placed there anyway. It took fourteen months, but after enough time away from his new "friends," Carter regained his previous perspective on life and returned to the family. Carter is now a senior in high school and appears to have given up his rebellion.

Only time will tell of course, but Carter's family is happy with their son and he seems happy to be back.

Manipulatory tough kids

Families are made up of people of varying ages who fill several roles at one time. Parents are providers, love-givers, disciplinarians, teachers, models, and friends.

Children and teens occupy an equally diverse pattern of roles, including parental supporters, mom's special kid, dad's special kid, love-givers, and challengers. Manipulatory tough kids attempts to use this family system to their advantage. Shauna was a manipulative tough kid.

This teenager was in an all-out war with her parents for control of her life. She was willing to threaten them with anything and everything she believed would scare them enough to make them give in to her unreasonable demands. Shauna had been dad's special kid at one time, and was consciously trying to use that status to get to him.

Under the surface, Shauna was probably very frightened. She may have been challenging her parents to see if they were strong enough to help her grow up.

No one knows for sure, but this thirteen year old was not responding well to anything. Her manipulations were working to the extent that her parents had not really been willing to do anything necessary to help this young teenager.

Dealing with the manipulatory tough kid

Because Shauna was only thirteen when all this was going on, the problem was just a little easier to resolve. After counseling with her parents, it was agreed that Shauna would be brought into the office for a joint session with her parents. I would conduct the session; the goal was to persuade Shauna that her life would get significantly more difficult if she failed to acknowledge her parents' control over her life.

Prior to the session, I gathered all the names of placement facilities so we could refer to them if needed. I contacted local and state psychiatric hospitals specializing in teen suicide prevention and treatment for serious depression and had several of the forms on the desk with their names clearly visible. I also encouraged Shauna's parents to be absolutely silent about what the session was going to cover. They were to act as though there was no problem, just for the few days until the family session.

When they came in that Thursday evening for their appointment, Shauna seemed as unhappy and defiant as ever. This was certainly not unexpected.

We got right down to business. I told Shauna that her parents were willing to do anything possible to help her and that we had agreed that some form of hospitalization might be necessary. Before Shauna could respond, I went on to describe the possibilities in case of a suicide attempt or another episode of running away. Shauna listened while staring alternately at the floor and at her father who did not wilt to her glare. It was clear that her parents had made up their mind that something was going to change at home.

I explained to her that this was being planned only as a contingency, that at the moment we were not sure that this was necessary. It was up to her to tell us, through her behavior, what she wanted us to do for her.

I encouraged her mom and dad to resist the temptation to remind their daughter how much they loved her. Shauna knew this of course, and now she needed to see some strength

51

and resolve to balance out the love she was taking for granted.

The session concluded with no commitment from Shauna, but we really had not asked her for one. She needed to know that her part in the decision was only through her behavior and nothing else. These were parents she was dealing with, and when you are thirteen years old, some decisions are made for you by your parents.

Though I am abbreviating this story somewhat, Shauna's behavior did improve enough so that she did not need to be placed. She did not run away again, and all talk of suicide stopped. Her parents watch her closely for setbacks—and will continue to do so for some time—perhaps until she is grown.

It has now been two years, and Shauna, at fifteen, seems a relatively normal Christian kid who is only slightly more difficult to raise than others.

We'll see what the future brings with this formerly manipulative tough kid.

The fearful, anxious tough kid

Anyone who has spent time with tough kids realizes the frequency of fear in their lives. Many difficult kids have been abused in some way and have been given the sense that they are unwanted, and therefore unloved. It can be argued that this is an unwarranted fear. The reality, though, is that *what is felt is real to the one who is feeling it.*

Fearful kids are afraid, even though it may be difficult or impossible to determine the source of their anxieties. When frightened, humans have two choices. We can run, or we can stand and fight. Evolutionists call this the "flight or fight response."

Many tough kids are running away from or fighting

against a threat that is real to them. Tough kids who are more inclined to be passive are likely to turn to drugs, alcohol, or even suicide, as a way of escaping their fears. Other tough kids will stand and fight their real or imagined enemy, even though they usually do not understand the nature of their enemy. Christian kids can be frightened like any kid of course.

But the things they are afraid of are often unique when compared to the world in general.

Kids from Christian families may be frightened of failing spiritually and disgracing their family. Others may fear failing to live up to the expectations of their parents in many areas of life: sports, school elections, popularity, making the cheerleading squad or the theatrical production coming up. Christian kids fear being embarrassed by the world.

But they also fear embarrassing their Lord and Savior. Christian kids fear that the negativism in so many church pulpits will come true in their lives, and they will live short of the potential others think they have. Christian kids, like all kids, fear that they will simply not measure up.

Dealing with the fearful, anxious tough kid

None of the three kids discussed in this chapter fit this category, but scores of others do. Options are limited, but effective. Counseling or psychotherapy with a licensed Christian counselor or psychologist will enable fearful tough kids to uncover the source of their fears, face them in the daylight, and learn of the unconditional acceptance of God.

How so many of our kids miss this truth I am not sure. It is easy to blame others, I suppose. But our challenge is to get these fearful kids in to see a trained person who can conduct spiritual-based counseling in an accepting environment and replace fear with unconditional love.

What do we recommend for the fearful kid?

The best thing is counseling or therapy with a trained professional counselor who understands the Bible and has successfully applied it to his or her own life. Jesus spoke words of power when He said: "I have told you these things, so that in me you may have peace. In this world you will have trouble. But take heart! I have overcome the world" (John 16:3).

The tough kid reacting to tough circumstances

Allen, the boy who saw his father beat his mother on the front lawn, seems to fit into this category. Psychologists call Allen's behavior a "situational emotional reaction."

It had its beginning in his parents' problems, and would probably stay with Allen for life, though he need not continue to suffer the reactions he had experienced.

But for Allen, the problem continued longer than it should because a messy divorce and custody battle kept his anger at the boiling point. Because Allen's parents did not end their battles when they ended their marriage, Allen continued to be exposed to his mother's constant criticism about his father. And when he was with his father, all he heard were comments about what a lousy wife his mother made. As is all too often the case, his parents put their own need to justify themselves above Allen's need to see both of them as good people who still loved him and would care for him.

Allen was expressing anger at the world for what had happened to him. Because he was only six at the time, his ability to understand and be counseled was limited by the constant bickering going on between his parents. His anger reflected his fear about who would care for him in an emergency or if one or the other parents became sick or died.

At six years of age, Allen needed adults to do for him what

he could not do for himself: protect him and make him feel secure.

Dealing with the situationally reactive tough kid

This kid needs help from other people. Even kids much older than Allen have difficulty changing their home situation, neighborhood, or school. Allen is helpless to do anything about his anger until his parents quit fighting with each other in front of their son.

Countless children and adolescents are misbehaving and getting into sometimes serious trouble. It's not that they want to. They just don't know how else to respond to the world adults have created for them. Often in cases such as Allen's, the child or teen can be helped by living for a time with other relatives.

Perhaps with time, Allen's mom and dad will realize what their adult behavior is doing to their small son. But until then, Allen may be better off living with grandparents for a while.

You may know youngsters struggling to deal with pain they do not understand. For those of us in a position to help, we can start by trying to change the problem situation in some way. If that does not succeed, we then consider alternate living arrangements for a time, until the situation clears itself up.

Ultimately, charges of neglect or emotional abuse may be lodged against the adults involved so that they will be motivated to stop involving the child in their adult problems. No easy answer exists for kids like Allen, but there are difficult answers which can be implemented if we can find adults courageous enough to try them.

We have looked at three tough kids in this chapter, each one a real living child or teen whose name has been changed to protect his or her privacy. As I reflect on these three tough kids, I am impressed with how much they depend on adults in their world for help with their problems. Yes, adults have usually caused or magnified the problem behaviors of these kids.

But just as adults are sometimes involved in creating the problem, many of the same adults can be involved in finding a solution.

Will the problem behavior continue?

Good parents are always good diagnosticians. Each parent knows the child better than anyone else on earth, and no expert is as much an expert as mom and dad. Granted, sometimes getting the information out is difficult, but no one knows the child better than that child's own parents.

With this in mind, I want us to look at ways of diagnosing continued problem behavior, even into adulthood. What must parents know about our kids in order to come to a decision regarding the level of their problem behavior? What kind of help should we provide for them? How do we know if we are dealing with future, as well as present, tough kids? And how can we tell if our semi-tough, tough, or super-tough kids will become semi-tough, tough, or super-tough adults?

Certain factors can give us the answer to the future behavior of problem kids. Here are some questions to ask about tough kids:

1. *How old was the child when the problem behavior began?* For most types of serious offenses, the younger the child when the behavior (stealing, fire setting, hurting pets) was first observed, the more serious the behavior is, and the more difficult it will be to correct. It is important to note that just growing up is a trial-and-error process for all children. The

challenge for parents is to be able to distinguish between more-or-less "normal" misbehavior, and behaviors such as those mentioned above.

2. How many different kinds of misbehavior have been observed?

Generally, the greater variety of serious misbehavior, the greater the problem and the more difficult the cure. Types of unacceptable behaviors include both the behaviors themselves and the situations in which they occur. A child or teen who engages in serious misbehavior only at home is assumed to be in somewhat better shape than another child who commits the same acts both at home and at school. We are therefore interested in how many different kinds of misbehavior have occurred and in how many different types of situations. The greater the number of each, the higher level of difficulty in treating the child or teenager.

3. How often has the misbehavior occurred?

Frequency is another important issue in enabling parents and others to determine the treatment needed by their child or teen. Unacceptable behaviors are always unwanted of course, but those that take place within a brief time span usually indicate a crisis approaching. Misbehaviors spread out over time, though still serious and in need of attention, may nevertheless not be of a crisis or immediate nature.

4. How serious was the misbehavior?

Remember Darrell and the deceased family cat? Clearly, Darrell's behavior is in a totally different category than Suzanne, the tantrum artist, or Robert, who would not obey his parents without grumbling.

It is not appropriate for me to imply that parents are wrong who insist that the misbehavior of their child or teen is not serious. However, professionals in the field who work with tough kids on a daily basis tend to limit the term "serious" to those behaviors that involve destruction of property (fire, vandalism) or violence against self or others. All misbehavior needs attention, but "serious" misbehavior needs more attention—and it needs that attention quickly.

5. What kinds of other behaviors are parents also noticing?

There tends to be a pattern of "symptoms" that accompany unacceptable behavior in seriously disturbed children and teens. These behaviors can be thought of as those related to (1) an uncontrollable urge, or compulsion, to commit a misdeed, and (2) physical and behavioral characteristics that, while not misbehavior in themselves, still upset parents.

For example, a child or teen who tells lies to try and get out of trouble is in one category. But a child or teen who lies for no apparent reason and seems to be unable to control his or her lying is in another, more serious, category. Similarly, a child who is misbehaving and also seems to be growing more and more careless about his or her appearance, cleanliness, and clothing, is in a more serious category as well.

6. What are parents and other family members like?

There is no guarantee that Christian parents and other family members will be spared from sinful or mentally unhealthy behavior. We are just as vulnerable as anyone to the effects of sin and the barbs thrown at us by evil forces.

Children and teens being raised by parents who are themselves psychologically or spiritually unhealthy will have additional hurdles to clear in growing up healthy. We know that in the families of seriously misbehaving kids, family factors enable and encourage the continuation of that misbehavior—even though the parents seem to want the misconduct stopped.

Perhaps mom's and dad's marriage is not going well. Kids are very good at sensing something like this, and any given kid may react to the possibility that his or her family may dissolve by becoming a "tough kid." In some cases, this is done to punish the parents for *their* misbehavior. In other cases, it may be done in the hope that running away or shoplifting and getting arrested will get mom and dad to pay attention to the needs of the kids in the family and make their marriage work.

Into the looking glass

Have you seen yourself or your family in these examples? Are you feeling better or worse than you did when you began this chapter? I know that I see parts of myself in every family I counsel. And I see myself in every individual tough child or teenager who walks through my office door.

I was a moderately tough kid as a teenager. You probably were too, though your parents probably had a different name for you when you got into trouble.

Do you remember?

"Disgrace to the family!"

"You must have been adopted, because no one in this family has ever done that before!"

"Thorn in my flesh!"

We don't need to go on. It just gets more depressing to remember unpleasant experiences from our past.

But we made it, didn't we? And if we continue to seek God's guidance and wisdom as parents, our tough kids will probably make it too.

If trouble continues, however, we can remind ourselves that *these children do not belong to us.* The problem did not begin with us and will not end with us. Children are loaned to us parents for a brief time of child-rearing, and ultimately, they alone will answer for their misbehavior.

We can pray and work for our kids, but they will stand before God one day with only the Lord Jesus to defend them, and there is no better lawyer.

The challenge of this chapter is for you to become a better diagnostician for your child's behavior. My goal has been to provide information so parents can better understand the degree of toughness they are dealing with.

I hope these challenges and goals have been attained. We have much more to discuss.

4

Super-Tough Kids

Super tough kids enter families well disguised as normal children. It is often only years later that they will be correctly diagnosed as seriously troubled. In this chapter we will examine the most common explanations for why tough kids become "tough" in the first place.

Parents will need to carefully consider the need of their children to be examined and evaluated for conditions that might be beyond their parental ability to deal with, and to learn how to help their children. The Whitcomb family is typical of families with a super tough kid. In this case, the super tough kid was named Danny.

Danny was born into the Whitcomb family on a January morning in 1981. The labor and delivery were exceptionally long and difficult. Though not premature, Danny was "light for dates," meaning that at five-and-a-quarter pounds, he weighed less than he should for a full-term baby boy.

Danny quickly gained a reputation as a "difficult" baby. He was fussy and unpredictable. He did not eat or sleep on any kind of regular schedule. The nurses commented that this

61

baby was totally unpredictable in terms of when a diaper change would be necessary. Even in his very earliest days, some suspected that Danny was being intentionally uncooperative.

Some of Danny's problems were related to a heart condition discovered on his six-week examination, a condition that required surgery and a long hospital stay beginning at six months and continuing for nearly a year. Of course Danny's parents were with him almost constantly during this time and his mother spent the night in his room on weekends.

Later, Danny's parents shared their typically mixed feelings with me. They were relieved to find that some or all of Danny's fussiness could have been caused by his heart condition, but they were worried about how their son would respond to surgery and being in a hospital for such a long time.

The Whitcombs had reason to be concerned.

Danny recovered fully from the surgery, and was able to return to his home as expected. He had a lot of medicine to take for the next few years and his physical activities would have to be closely monitored, but other than that, Danny was physically in good shape.

But this youngster was already beginning to let people know that he was not in good shape otherwise. Although it would be a long time before Danny's parents could admit to themselves that their son was different, the evidence was becoming unavoidable.

Their son exhibited an apparently uncontrollable temper in all situations. He was different from Jamie Wilson, who simply tried to manipulate his environment with his behavior. Danny, beginning at age three, was prone to explosive and violent outbursts without provocation or warning. His parents once described him as a "nuclear kid," always close to meltdown.

Because Danny was the first child for the Whitcombs, they made a classic error in dealing with Danny's behavior. They began to bribe, spoil, and otherwise over-indulge this pre-schooler, a parental choice that led to Danny's first truly violent act when he was only five years old.

He was caught trying to set fire to his house after a particularly nasty temper tantrum (which had been followed by a very rare spanking). Danny had been sent to his room, where he had hidden away a book of matches. It was only the sounding of the smoke detector in his room that saved the home, and probably Danny's life.

At this point, Danny was formally evaluated at a child guidance clinic and found to be an emotionally troubled child. This was the first time that the Whitcombs heard the term, "unattached child"—but it would not be the last.

The critical first year

Therapists use the terms "bonding" and "attachment" interchangeably to describe the process of forming a connection between primary caregiver (usually the mother) and the infant. This process follows a predictable cycle. First, the infant experiences a need of some kind—hunger, thirst, or physical discomfort. This need produces a form of anger in the infant commonly described as "rage." The rage leads the baby to cry, fuss, and in other ways try to let others know that this nearly helpless human being is in need of something.

Following the expression of rage, the infant experiences the mother or father coming to them and meeting the need they are feeling at the time. A change of diaper, warm bottle of milk, or a hug and some attention lead the infant to feel a reduction of both the need and the rage over feeling the need in the first place. Once the infant experiences gratification of need, they slowly learn to trust the person or persons who met their need.

So the process begins with the infant feeling a need, becoming angry and expressing rage over having the need, then experiencing gratification and relief at the hands of parents or other caregivers, and finally coming to trust that future needs will be met in the same way. Now think with me about this process and Danny Whitcomb.

Danny was hospitalized very early in the sequence I described above. That was certainly no one's fault, but it was a difficult situation nevertheless. Because Danny was separated from his mother at this critical time and placed in the care of others, he undoubtedly experienced needs that were not met as they would have been at home with Mom. Hospital personnel usually do an excellent job of caring for children, but no one would claim that they provide the same level of care as children can get at home.

So Danny experienced needs and the rage that always accompanies such needs, but did not experience gratification and relief as he would have at home. Because he sometimes had to wait for his needs to be met and his rage to be reduced, Danny probably failed to develop the sense of trust in both his environment *and* his parents.

Failure to develop trust is the same as failure to attach or bond. Such failure to trust and form attachments can be caused by post-partum depression in the mother, natural catastrophe requiring parents and children to be apart, parents returning to work too soon, or as with Danny, being hospitalized and separated from a responsive care-giver.

This process of attachment is the most commonly accepted explanation for the difficulty in adopting children older than a few months, and is probably what happened with Darrell, who was also premature, and Juan, who was adopted out of unknown circumstances at age five. We would expect the same might be true of children who are neglected or abused, passed from foster home to foster home, or who experience any other form of instability related to a primary care-giver.

Could this child be yours?

The unattached or "unbonded" child, like Danny, has not developed the most basic sense of attachment to one or both parents for any number of reasons. In Danny's case, the more than eleven months he stayed in the hospital as a baby was strongly suspected of being the cause behind his emotional instability and explosiveness. Psychologists who evaluated Danny concluded that this was the most reasonable explanation for his apparent failure to bond, but they emphasized to the Whitcombs that an answer is never an absolute with children like their son.

Children who suffer from this condition display a specific and observable set of behaviors. We will deal with each in this chapter and relate them to specific age groups in later chapters.

This is an overview of typical behavior of unattached, unbonded children. But remember, children can fail to bond and attach for a number of reasons other than those experienced by Danny Whitcomb.

Behaviors to look for

1. Self-destructiveness and extreme risk-taking.
Danny was known for engaging in what his parents called "dare-devil behavior." He would think nothing of climbing

the highest ladder and trying to balance on one foot on top of the garage. At one point he was seen to be standing on one foot at the end of the boat dock attached to the family vacation cottage, despite repeated warnings about drowning. Many children like Danny also have an extreme tolerance for pain, especially if it is self-inflicted or experienced on one of the dare-devil adventures. Children who are unbonded may be normal in complaining about a small scratch, but might not tell parents about a serious injury for days—and apparently not experience much pain either.

It seems as though these children are unable to admit that they can be injured or that they may need help from others. In extreme cases of abuse or neglect, head-banging and other forms of self-destructiveness are often observed. Self-destructiveness and extreme risk-taking are not the traits of normal children and should not be written off as "boys will be boys," or simply "having courage."

2. *Resistance to control and discipline.*

Unattached and unbonded children cannot tolerate others putting restraints or controls on them. Just as these children resisted being held and cuddled as infants, they now resist with equal ferocity any attempts to discipline them or convince them that they should behave. Children like Danny have the ability to control themselves, and will do so when it suits them—but only when it suits them! They will attempt to control situations when they are with outsiders, such as when adults are engaged in a conversation and the child is not included.

You can expect that the rage at being ignored will build and the child will find some way of sabotaging the adults' conversation and becoming the center of attention—even if only for a moment.

When working with a family such as Danny's, the

counseling problem that brings them to the office will be centered on discipline, and several distinctives about discipline will stand out. The child will be described as "very bad," and examples will abound. Also, parents will claim to have "tried everything" to no avail. This is often true. The child will be described as engaging in very serious misbehavior such as violence or fire-setting and much of the misbehavior will be of the risky type mentioned above. Finally, the child specialist and parents will fail in finding any short-term or simple solution to the child's non-compliance. Spanking absolutely will not be effective with a child like this.

3. *Inability to give or receive affection.*

As infants, unbonded children squirm and arch their back when held, seem to prefer a bottle in their crib to being fed while held, and resist affectionate behavior such as hugs and kisses. As the child grows ar ⌐ the behavior continues, parents usually feel that they have done something wrong, that they have offended this youngster in some way. What is really going on is that the child is simply protecting the self against the kind of unmet need he or she experienced as a younger child. The thought pattern seems to be, "I must keep others at a distance so that I cannot be hurt again."

4. *Cruelty to pets or other children, especially younger children.*

The story of Darrell and the family cat is repeated in countless families of unbonded children. Family pets become targets because of their helplessness and their inability to tell. So it is with younger children in the neighborhood, including younger brothers and sisters of the unattached child. These children are not only cruel, but sneaky and careful in their cruelty. Everything is blamed on an "accident," or another child who is usually unavailable to defend himself.

"Accidental" pushes down stairs at school or the closing of a door on a younger child's fingers are blamed on simple accidents—or on the other child for not being careful enough. The energy behind the offending child's defenses often makes it difficult for some parents and others to continue to suspect that the "accident" was intentional.

5. *Preoccupation with fire, blood, gore, and dark colors.* Unbonded children are angry at the world. Though unaware of the reason for their strong feelings, these children are in fact, just plain angry.

Drawings and stories made up by these children will focus on themes of death, destruction, and mutilation, often to such an extent that the family cannot believe such aggressive and hurtful thoughts could be coming out of such a young child.

From earliest days, the unattached child believes he is bad and, because he is evil, he must constantly battle the forces of good. Parents of these children will often find a secret collection of terrible drawings depicting violent themes. Parents will find cut-out pictures from newspapers and magazines of murder and accident victims, along with underlined descriptions of what happened to them.

"I am bad," the unattached, unbonded child thinks. "I don't know why or how I got this way, but I know it is true." This kind of thinking leads this child as he grows to confirm what he believes are the expectations of others and he will be bad— and apparently enjoy the notoriety that follows when he is revealed as a "bad" person.

6. *Lack of friends.*

All through the growing years, these children will experience a conspicuous absence of long-term childhood friends. The reality is simply that it is very difficult to fool children, and other kids will sense something wrong after a while. Without necessarily knowing why, they will stop coming around to play. It is important for parents to be able to distinguish between casual, "acquaintance"-type friends and long-term friends. Many of these children are junior con-artists and can fool children and adults until others get to know them. Parents should be alert to this and use it as a key diagnostic tool in evaluating children who may be in this category.

7. *Learning disorders and disabilities.*

Unbonded children do not deal well with authority figures at any level, from parents to teachers to police. Because of this, they do not do well in school. Typically diagnosed as "marginally disabled educationally," these children quickly gain reputations as troublemakers and poor students. But note that this has nothing at all to do with intelligence. Troubled kids are found in all intelligence categories. Some will have formally diagnosed learning disabilities like dyslexia and hyperactivity, while others will be informally diagnosed as simply "problem children."

8. *Failure to make normal eye contact.*

Unattached children do not feel connected to others in a way that allows normal interpersonal behavior. One of the most obvious manifestations of this is eye contact. Unattached and unbonded infants are noticed for their resistance to "gazing," the normal looking into one another's eyes common to mother and child. As toddlers and preschoolers they will try to turn their head away, close their eyes, and actively fight looking into someone's eyes. As older children and teenagers they may let hair down over their eyes or wear sunglasses. Girls may even resort to very heavy eye makeup as a way to keep others from looking into their eyes, or from having to look into the eyes of other people.

9. *Phoniness.*

"Robot-like" is the way one mother described her ten-year-old son. It was as if he was trying to act the part of a child and not really knowing how to do it right. Other terms applied to these children include "plastic," "artificial," and "unreal." Unattached children do not have an "internal self" to provide intuition and feedback on how others see them and how they should respond. Because of this, they feel as unreal as others see them, but lack the ability to both recognize what it is that's troubling them as well as how to deal with it. These kids know there is something wrong, but in themselves, are lost about what to do about it.

10. *Superficial friendliness with strangers.*

Unbonded children will not resist being picked up by strangers, even as babies when "stranger anxiety" is supposed to be developing. This characteristic may be what starts many unbonded children on the road to being good "con artists." They learn that a happy smile will fool many adults. Of course, people in daily contact with the child quickly learn that there is something different about this child; the apparent friendliness and cooperation are really manipulative tactics designed to allow the child to get his or her way. These children are often described as "precocious" socially. In fact, this behavior is a manifestation of early learning of how to get their way with adults.

11. *Stealing.*

Unbonded and unattached children do not empathize with others. Because they do not seem able to imagine what it must feel like to have a toy or other favorite item taken by someone, they will steal and feel absolutely no remorse for their behavior. When caught, they will be sorry and express repentance, but the repentance is for being caught, not for stealing. Stealing will also occur in conjunction with compulsiveness, leading the child to many, many experiences of getting in trouble for "dumb" stealing. They may take something right in front of another person, almost as if they wanted to get caught. In fact, it is this compulsiveness that is sometimes seen as bravado or "guts" that further confuses parents and teachers.

"Of course he didn't mean to steal it," argues mom to the teacher. "Look how obvious he was in letting himself be seen." The child did not want to get caught, but his compulsiveness and lack of empathy simply allowed him to grab what he wanted.

12. *Crazy lying.*

Unbonded kids lie all the time, not just once in a while. They lie for convenience and for necessity. And most distinctively, they lie in the face of reality, when caught red-handed. If asked to explain why he took the cookie that is now in his hand, the unbonded child may look up at the parent and ask "What cookie?"

Unbonded children seem to have an almost unlimited ability to see the world and their situation as they wish it was rather than as it actually is. No lie detection machine can tell when an unbonded child or adult is lying because they can persuade themselves that fantasy has become reality. Such an ability also helps explain why there is such an absence of true remorse or repentance when they're caught. One only need observe the behavior of adults in this category to see how pervasive this trait can become.

13. *Parents pushed to their limit.*

To have an unattached and unbonded child is to face the greatest challenge any parent could face. These children are intelligent, but apparently lacking in conscience; disciplined, but failing to learn from the discipline; loved, but unable to accept or return the love; fearful of what lies ahead, but unable to determine how they will deal with the future.

Parents of these children need great amounts of help and support from family and friends. Most of all they need to be understood—understood as good parents struggling against a monumental problem in a small package. They are loving parents of an unloving child, caregivers entrusted with the most difficult child imaginable, and parents facing a lifetime of limited successes in child-rearing. Parents of these "tough kids" need all the help we can give them!

Facing the challenge

Unbonded and unattached children are not beyond helping, but that aid must occur early in the child's life if it is to work. The emphasis in this chapter has been on diagnosis, helping parents decide if a child needs to be examined by a professional who can prescribe a treatment plan. *Under no circumstances should a decision to treat a child be made without a careful examination in a licensed child-care facility by licensed professionals.*

With this caution in mind, I would like to explore two common treatment methods for use with unattached and unbonded children, but I say again, such treatment must never be undertaken by parents themselves or by others lacking proper training and credentials. My purpose in including this information is simply to leave you with a greater sense of optimism than you may have to this point. These children can be helped, but with difficulty and limited degrees of success. And they must be helped *early* in life!

Treatment examples

"Rage Reduction Therapy" is one method used with children diagnosed as unattached and unbonded. The process, greatly simplified here, is for the child therapist and a few staff assistants to work as a team. The child lies on his back across a row of pillows on the laps of several assistants who are assigned to gently hold the child's arms or legs. The child is then tickled and encouraged to become angry, to experience the "rage" believed to be at the center of his problem with life.

The child does become enraged, and would be out of control except that he is held and cannot move. This process is experienced in waves of tension so the child has the opportunity to relax from time to time. The child is tickled and held, tickled and held until he is willing to say something like "Okay, I know you are the boss. I have to do what you say."

The point of rage reduction therapy is to teach the child what he failed to learn, that he must do what parents and some other adults tell him to. It seems like such an obvious treatment, but what this child has failed to learn is that the world is populated with people who can and will make him do things. If we can teach him this at a young age, he might be prevented from getting into the kind of adult trouble that makes the newspapers.

This treatment, and the one to follow, are not to be undertaken by parents. Only a trained professional with proper credentials should be allowed to attempt rage reduction therapy.

Rage reduction therapy is a new treatment method. Long-term benefits and side-effects have not been clearly established. But in spite of the possible dangers, this method has helped many super tough kids.

The second treatment method applied to super tough kids is known by several names, the most common of which is "Dependency Therapy."

As with rage reduction therapy, dependency therapy must only be attempted by parents carefully trained by clinical experts. This method is practiced at home. It involves the parents insisting that the disobedient, uncooperative, possibly destructive child become dependent again on his parents, to the point of becoming almost an infant again.

The child—and this will only work with children still physically small enough to be restrained and forced to do what parents demand—is required to ask for everything he or she wants or needs. These children cannot take a drink of water alone. They cannot go to the bathroom without permission and assistance. They have no more privileges or power than a six-month-old infant would have. In much the same way that some learning disabled children are forced to crawl in order to establish correct brain pathways that did not form properly, these tough kids are required to crawl through life for as many months as it takes for them to recognize their total dependence on their parents.

That part of the learning curve that was originally missed for some reason is now taught again. Some have called this "remedial socialization." The process is similar to that of a child enrolled in a remedial reading class who is required to learn reading at the five-year-old level even though the child may be ten years old.

Let me emphasize again, these methods are employed by parents and child professionals who have had special training in one or both of these methods. Parents must never try to attempt them on their own. There are dangers involved in such radical methods, and though success rates are encouraging, damage is always possible.

What happened to Danny Whitcomb?

We don't know the end of the story yet. I know that Danny is nine years old, and that he spent about seven months living away from his family when he was six-and-a-half years old.

He is in twice-a-week therapy with a child psychologist, and attends a special class for emotionally disturbed children in a public school near his home. His parents have told mutual friends they are satisfied with his progress. Time will tell of course, but Danny will likely continue to be a challenge to his parents and others for some time. Maybe for all his life.

A reminder for Christian parents

This chapter is not the most "spiritual" in this book. As is often the case when dealing with really difficult problems, there is a lot to be understood before parents can know what it is that God would have us do.

What we have been discussing in this chapter is how to diagnose a child who is seriously troubled and possibly dangerous. The material is not pleasant to read or to apply. But the need is obvious. Our job as Christian parents is to find a way to deal with the children God has "loaned" us for a few years of child rearing. The limitations we see in these tough kids did not begin with parents, nor will they end with parents. In most cases, we neither caused nor contributed to the dilemma faced by tough kids.

But we are involved, of course. And there are many things we can do to help them. The most important is early detection. What we can do before God and man is resist the temptation to surrender our children to themselves, to allow them to slip away into a troubled life without doing everything we can to help. It is still the job of Christian parents to make it as easy as possible for children like Danny to do right, and to make it as hard as possible for them to do wrong.

But in the final analysis, parents can only do so much. We must agree with the Prophet Isaiah: "He shall gather the lambs with his arms, and carry them into his bosom" (Isa.40:11).

God is ultimately in charge of these tough children!

5

High-Risk Families

Families can be placed in a high risk category for a number of reasons. The parents may be criminal in orientation, cultic in their religion, or mentally ill. They may be neglectful or abusive, sexually exploitive, drug or alcohol addicted, or simply absent. Families with these characteristics are usually known to school personnel, the police, social welfare agencies, and child protective services. Parents like these cannot hide what is happening to their children and themselves; eventually the situation explodes and the family collapses.

But I want us to consider a different kind of high-risk family, one that you and I are very likely to see in the churches we attend and in the neighborhoods where we live. These high-risk families do not look like they are at risk for anything bad—until you get to know them.

The Carswell Family

Bill and Aletha Carswell met in Bible college where Bill was studying for the pastorate. He was a senior, and Aletha was a freshman studying to be a teacher. Her parents were concerned about the four-year age difference, but they liked Bill very much and were thrilled that their youngest daughter was marrying a minister.

As soon as Bill graduated, they married. He was 22, she was 18. The children came along quickly. By the time they were in their early thirties, the Carswell family was complete, with two boys and a baby sister.

Upon graduation, Bill took a succession of associate pastor positions, and by age 45, he was the senior pastor of a relatively large church in Pennsylvania. It averaged nearly 1,500 in attendance at the morning worship service.

Aletha, though having finished her education after marrying Bill, had not taught school or worked outside the home at all. Her husband believed that wives should remain at home and care for the children, who were now nearly all grown.

Scott, the oldest at 22, no longer lived at home. His younger brother, Wesley was 20, and Gail was 17.

The Carswell family was indeed complete—but as I would soon learn, being complete and being healthy are very different matters. There were cracks in the foundation of this family that would threaten to bring down all they had worked so long to accomplish.

The Foundation Trembles

Bill had become very well known in the north central region of Pennsylvania through the daily radio program emanating from his church.

He was a gifted speaker, and the broadcast had helped the church grow to capacity in the few years since he had become senior pastor. He was burdened about family concerns, and spoke often on the needs of the Christian family. In much demand, Bill Carswell had more invitations to speak to Christian groups than he could accept.

Things were going about as well for Bill as he could wish. So the blow he experienced when his oldest son, Scott, left school was even more severe because it was so unexpected.

Scott, 22, announced to his parents that he was leaving the Christian college and taking a job in a distant city. His plans to live in Atlanta and not complete college were a total surprise to his father, and could not have caused more disruption to the family.

Bill simply would not hear of it. He became angry in a way that no one in the family had seen before and, to use Scott's term, Bill "lost it"!

An additional blow came when Scott told his parents he had broken up with the girl everyone assumed he would soon marry.

Everything seemed to be in chaos for Bill.

Scott moved to Atlanta and took a sales job with a publishing firm. Letters home became less frequent and phone calls grew noticeably awkward. Bill and Aletha became worried that there was something that Scott wasn't telling them about his life. They were right!

The following semester, Wesley was placed on academic probation because of falling grades. The counseling center called, with Wesley's permission, to tell the Carswells that their son was being treated for depression. In fact, he might need to come home for more intense therapy if he did not improve very soon.

No suicidal thinking had been discovered, but it was clear that the college administration was worried about Wesley.

Gail, a senior in high school, did not appear to be "cracking" like her brothers, but her behavior at home was growing more and more "independent," and her father was beginning to worry about the fine line between independence and rebellion.

His daughter, like most others her age, insisted on choosing her own dates, and seemed to challenge even the most minor rules. Bill knew that Gail's behavior and attitudes warranted "keeping an eye on her."

The Cracks Begin to Show

The bombshell arrived in the mail. Scott sent his parents a letter telling them that he would not be coming home at Christmas as they had expected. He had moved in with a "roommate," a young man named Jerrold who he worked with. Both Bill and Aletha knew instinctively that their son was telling them that he was homosexual.

A phone call to Scott that evening confirmed their suspicions.

"Devastation" does not adequately describe the depth of despair in the Carswell home. The next weeks and months were unbearably dark, and only their faith kept them going. Bill offered to resign his pastorate but the offer was not even considered by the church board. Bill was deep into "self-blame," and insisted that he was somehow at fault for what his grown son had decided to do.

Wesley was told about his brother and took it better than his folks expected. Even more surprising, his grades began to improve slowly, and he reported feeling better.

While Wesley was less upset than his parents expected, his sister, Gail, reacted more outspokenly. Mostly in anger, Gail's feelings were directed at her father. At one point, she accused her father of pushing Scott into this homosexual lifestyle through the unreasonably high expectations of the "first born son." She also charged that Bill, a typical Christian workaholic, had spent very little time with his children, leaving the "child-rearing" up to Aletha.

Here we have the Carswell family—Christian, conservative, Bible-believing, an intact family unit, church attenders, tithers—by any normal criteria a "good" family.

But something was going terribly wrong, and was going to go even more wrong before things improved.

Bill Carswell eventually surrendered his pastorate and left the ministry completely.

Following his resignation from the ministry, Bill and Aletha separated and divorced. She finally became a teacher.

Wesley struggled with depression, but graduated from college and did reasonably well.

Gail attended a secular university where she met, and married, a man from a totally different religious background. Before long, they divorced, and Gail moved back to be closer to her mother. The two have become more like friends now than mother and daughter.

What Went Wrong?

How can a family look so good and still self-destruct?

Before we try to answer that question about the Carswell family, let's remember a few things.

First, parental mistakes and environmental conditions beyond the person's control may impact an individual. But this does not mean that anyone is exempt from personal responsibility for actions taken as an adult, even a young adult. Scott may or may not have begun living a homosexual lifestyle because of the way his father treated him.

Usually, the true reason is never known with certainty.

But what we *do* know is that God holds each of us

responsible for our actions, regardless of the factors leading up to those actions. Paul, writing to the Galatian church, declared under inspiration of God: "Do not be deceived: God cannot be mocked. A man reaps what he sows. The one who sows to please his sinful nature, from that nature will reap destruction; the one who sows to please the Spirit, from the Spirit will reap eternal life" (Galatians 6:7-8).

Scott will answer for his adult sin—and so will his father for his adult sin. But where sin abounds, grace much more abounds.

In I John 1:9, we are reminded of what Scott and all other sinners need to do to obtain forgiveness. "If we confess our sins, he is faithful and just and will forgive us our sins and purify us from all unrighteousness."

By developing possible explanations for behaviors only God truly understands, I don't want to appear to be doing anything more than speculating. Many times we are correct in speculations such as these, but we are wrong at times too. Only God knows the heart. But perhaps we can understand some possible reasons for our children's undesirable behavior, and thereby avoid making future mistakes. None of us want the experiences that the Carswell family had.

To help readers avoid becoming like the Carswell family, I am suggesting some questions each parent should ask themselves about their family and the way they parent.

Questions:

1. *Are the parents warm and nurturant with the children and each other?*

Bill Carswell was described by everyone who knew him as a good man who wanted to do the right thing. But he also had the tendency to be critical, judgmental, and lacking in affection with the children. People who knew the family assumed that Bill was warmer in private than he was in public, but this turned out to be a false hope. He had been raised to believe that fathers revealed weakness when they showed affection, and even Aletha talked about how "unloved" she had felt throughout their marriage.

Bill, like so many Christian men (and men in general), confused sex with love. He believed that his sexual energies conveyed love to his wife. He was wrong!

I ask fathers in my counseling office (if I get the chance): "Why would any child want to be like a father who was never affectionate or nurturant?" Human beings want to be like people who like them and who let them know it.

"Of course I love my children" comes the gruff reply. "I feed them, don't I?"

This was not enough in Bill Carswell's case.

2. *Do the children depend upon their own parents to get their needs met?*

In the Carswell family, needs were met by mom, not dad. Yes, Bill was the income producer. But when the kids wanted something, they had to ask Aletha because dad was always at the church or out on calls. Why did Scott adopt a sexual orientation totally different from that of his father? Maybe because it was always mom who was nice and dad who was not. Who would want to imitate a person who provides only negative input in our lives? Scott may have developed a feminine orientation simply because the most important man in his young life was not very pleasant to be around.

When Gail was growing up and needed confirmation of her developing beauty, where was dad? Are we really surprised at her rebellion in high school and her even stronger rebellion in her first marriage? Isn't it possible that Gail was saying to her father, "Okay, Dad, you ignored me all those years when I needed you. Now just try to ignore this!"

Wesley, with his depression, could have been reacting in his own way to the unmet needs he had—needs for psychological and spiritual support he was not getting. Dad was critical, and mom was too weak to confront dad and protect the kids.

Wesley might have been depressed for no other reason than that he realized, down deep, that no one cared what happened to him.

3. *Are the standards of Christian living set by the parents clear and consistent?*

After the divorce of their parents, Wesley and Gail told me how they struggled as children to understand the contradictions in their parents' behavior. Dad would talk one way in the presence of others and another way at home. He was nicer to his wife in public than he was in private, but harder on his children in public than in private. It was very important to Bill that he be seen as a good disciplinarian, even though he was often inconsistent behind closed doors.

Bill, in other words, was a performance-oriented Christian.

He was interested in setting a good example for the people in his church—even if that example was to some degree false. Aletha's example was more consistent, but it wasn't one Gail wanted to emulate. Gail expressed how opposed she was to letting any man treat her as the "doormat" her mother had been all those years.

4. *Do the parents agree that they are models for their children?* One of the memories that stayed with Wesley and Gail (and we could assume the same for Scott although he wasn't involved in these discussions) was how their parents constantly stressed the need for the children to do better than their parents had done with their lives. It's a normal desire for parents to have for their children perhaps, but the memories the kids held were very different.

They interpreted these "encouragements" as statements of how unhappy their parents were with the lives they had chosen, and that they wanted their children to make better choices than they had made.

Clearly, Gail remembered, the message she got from her mother was to marry someone not in the ministry—and someone very different from Bill. This was subtle and unspoken of course, but Gail read the message loud and clear. Also, Aletha was not happy with staying home when the children were grown, and she was unhappy with Bill's unwillingness to compromise.

Wesley was impressed with his father's devotion to the ministry, but he was also strongly impressed with how negative his father was about the actual day-to-day aspects of ministry work. Bill had said on several occasions that he wished he could just be himself and not need to always "play the preacher" just to impress people. The message Wes received was that a minister must work hard to "fit the role" as his father described it, even if it meant being deceptive.

5. *Are the parents powerful people?*

No person, child or adult, would want to be weak, or imitate others who are weak. This will come as no surprise I'm sure. But it is surprising how often Christians seem to judge their spirituality by how much abuse they can take at the hands of the world.

Bill was a powerful preacher and had very good interpersonal skills, but the denomination to which they belonged was a "board-led" denomination. This meant that the minister did not have the last word on decisions affecting the church. Bill knew this, of course, but the family was very aware of how often he would come home and complain about being weaker than the board members, and that he was not really in charge of his own ministry.

The fact that this father needed to share his feelings of weakness with his family no doubt encouraged them to see their father as weak, and no child will want to become a weak person.

The real damage related to weakness involved Gail and her mother. Gail knew how much her mother wanted to teach and establish a career of her own. Everyone agreed that Aletha would make a great teacher. Yet Bill would not hear of it. From Gail's perspective, it was not love and submission that kept her mother at home and out of the classroom, but weakness. Gail perceived Aletha as too weak to stand up for herself. Regardless of how one feels on the issue of wives working, the perception of weakness was established.

It is speculative, but reasonable, to assume that parental weakness played a major part in the unwise decisions all three children made as they grew up and left home. Only after their parents had divorced did Gail and Scott sit down with their mother and talk about this.

Aletha thought she was teaching submission, but the message was received as one of simple weakness. Bill thought he was being a good Christian by giving in to the church board and saving his true opinions for the family, but he too was teaching weakness.

6. *How did the parents in the family relate to God?*

Parents are every child's first God. Each of us learns about the nature of God years before we are able to understand what we are learning.

Bill and Aletha were good Christians in many ways. But their unhappiness and dissatisfaction with the ministry led their children to understand that God might not be trusted to know what is best for us. After all, they grew up listening to their parents complain about the difficult ministry God had "given them." Why then, when it was the children's turn to seek a ministry from God, would they trust God anymore than their parents had?

What became of the Carswell family was not pleasant. If we are not careful, we could become as discouraged as they did. But what keeps Christian counselors and pastors going are the many successful Christian families who can raise their children well while preserving, even enhancing, their marriage.

We see too many examples of "functional" families in the church to believe that such good families are on the endangered species list. Threatened perhaps, but not to the point of being endangered. (At least not yet.)

So what have we learned about the "low-risk" Christian family, and how does this family compare with one like the Carswells?

Low-risk, stable, fully functioning Christian families

As with the traits in high-risk, dysfunctional families, low-risk functional traits are observed in degrees rather than absolutes.

We are examining relative proportion and not absolute numbers. We are examining families known to be more successful than unsuccessful, closer to satisfactory than unsatisfactory, and raising less disturbed children rather than more disturbed children.

Good family qualities, in other words, are not on either extreme of the good/bad continuum, but simply nearer the good end than the bad end. Functional doesn't mean perfect. There aren't any perfect families, because there aren't any perfect people. And there aren't any perfect people because God said there aren't. The degeneration of the world provides ample proof.

The point is that you and I are not to feel like failures because we are not perfect. If your family doesn't measure up on every one of the characteristics I am going to list, it just means that your family is like all families—imperfect!

1. *In fully functioning Christian families, problems are not only recognized and acknowledged, but resolved as well.*

Children learn most of what they know from observing their parents, and it is not only okay, but even good for the children to see mom and dad wrestling with a problem. But the kids also need to see mom and dad solving that problem.

We learn to be parents by being children, after all, and part of being a parent is having problems. It comes with the territory.

Now this doesn't mean that every problem your family faces will get solved. Many problems have no solution.

Imagine a family with a retarded child, or a parent who becomes permanently disabled, or a family that loses a parent or child to death. Problems like these have no answer, in the sense that nothing will change the reality of what has happened. But the fully functioning family will deal with the problem in a productive way, even though the situation cannot be altered.

2. *In the fully functioning, low-risk Christian family, all members of the family can express themselves.*

As you were growing up, were there people in your family you could not talk to? Did your family believe that "children should be seen and not heard"? Were there topics that could not be discussed out loud under any circumstances? Subjects like sex? Religion? Politics? Family relationships? Why mom and dad hardly talk to each other anymore?

The fully functioning Christian family is open to honest expression of feelings, thoughts, desires—even fantasies. And this kind of family is open to such expression without fear of retaliation or revenge from other family members. Of course, there are requirements to be polite and respectful, but in good families, nothing much is "off limits" under the right circumstances.

3. *All relationships in the fully functioning low-risk Christian family are on an equal basis.*

Each person in the family is of equal worth and value—even the smallest child or the eldest and most infirm grandparent. They have different responsibilities and privileges of course, but at the heart of the matter, everyone is the equal of everyone else.

We only need to turn to Paul's letter to the Galatian church where he reminded them of God's standards of equality. "There is neither Jew nor Greek, slave nor free, male nor female, for you are all one in Christ Jesus" (Galatians 3:28).

So when we consider the role of children in the family, we must remember the words of Jesus warning us about offending little ones or preventing children from coming to Him. Anyone who knows the Bible knows that children and young people have a special place of protection in the Savior's heart.

4. *In the fully-functioning Christian family, communication is direct, fearless, and spontaneous.*

In good families, each person, child or adult, feels free to talk with anyone else in the family. No one is "off limits" or too good to be bothered with the chatter of children. Communication is direct in that there are no obstacles or barriers in the way. It is fearless in that even the smallest children feel comfortable and unafraid of speaking their mind at the dinner table. And it is spontaneous because family members do not have to worry that what they say may be misinterpreted and come back to hurt them.

Communication is good only when any speaker can speak

to any listener, and any listener can respond to any one who speaks. With good communication, there are no barriers, no people too good or too busy to listen to the smallest child, no people unwilling to consider the viewpoint of the other. Communication in fully functioning families is built on trust rather than fear, self-confidence rather than self-reproach.

5. *In fully-functioning families, members can get their needs met.*

People of all ages seem to have three basic human needs. Each of us needs a sense of power, of worth, and of belonging.

God has ordained the family unit to supply these needs in the years when the child is too young to understand that God is ultimately the One who supplies what we need. Families therefore, and especially parents, have the responsibility to give children of all ages the feeling that their opinion is worth something. Even the youngest members of the family must feel they are worth asking what they might think about family business such as vacations, meals, and special events. Giving children a sense of power is more a matter of attitude than action. Parents who truly value their children will instinctively fulfill their power need.

A sense of worth is established in the earliest years by parents who pay attention to the child and who behave as though they value this child's contribution to the family. We call parents who do this "facilitators," those who instinctively work to convince the child that he or she is a bundle of potentialities in the process of becoming a great human being.

A sense of belonging is accomplished through parental attitudes communicating that the child is genuinely wanted by other family members. Those fortunate children will grow to believe that even if they were not born into this family, they would be welcomed anyway just because they are such great kids.

Evidence for the power of belonging can be seen sometimes in children who have been adopted or raised by foster parents. These kids, even though well taken care of in a physical and emotional sense, worry about what is so wrong with them that their original parents gave them up. It's totally irrational of course, but very common. Power, worth, and belonging. These are indispensable components of the fully functioning family.

6. *Differences are acknowledged and accepted in fully functioning families.*

Linda and I know a Christian family made up of mom and dad and five daughters. They're a very musical family. All five daughters play the violin, and when they perform, they wear identical dresses—even mom who plays the piano as accompaniment. This is a very nice family, but I have wondered what would have happened if one of those five daughters wanted to play the saxophone instead of the violin. Would she have been allowed to?

In fully functioning Christian families, children are not seen as part of a unit but as individuals within a unit. Family members are allowed, even encouraged, to be different—to show their uniqueness as creations of God. Parents in good families encourage the development of skills and aptitudes even though these abilities may not be what parents expected for their children. The idea is that parents recognize that God created children and He has a plan for their lives that can be expected to differ from the expectations of their human parents. If we understand God's sovereignty in this issue, we will be better able to accept the individuality of each child.

7. *In fully functioning Christian families, parents are self-disciplined disciplinarians.*

Parents expect from their children what they are willing to do themselves. Imagine the hypocrisy of an overweight mother telling her teenage children that they should control the amount of "junk" food they eat. Or the work-aholic father preaching to his son on the evils of watching too much television.

For a Christian, to be self-disciplined really means being "God-disciplined" in that we recognize the need to live a controlled life as we understand God's will for us.

I sometimes ask parents as we discuss their concerns with discipline if they yell at their children for yelling. Do they hit their child for hitting another child? I have known parents who actually bit their child to teach him or her not to bite other children. Does this show self-discipline by the parent? And what does the child learn from this? That it is okay to yell, hit, and bite—but only if you are a grown-up? I wonder!

8. In fully-functioning Christian families, roles within the family are voluntary and flexible.

It is no secret that family members assume certain roles, and do so at a very young age. One child may assume the role of "joker," or "happy child"—the one who can be counted on to try and cheer everyone up. Another child may become "dad's buddy" or "mom's pal." Others become a "winner," "hero," "athlete," or "the popular one."

In healthy, well-functioning families, these roles are voluntary and usually reflect a major characteristic of a child's personality. But in unhealthy families, roles tend to be forced upon children—roles such as "troublemaker," "poor student," "dad's anger target" or "mom's scapegoat."

These roles are almost always imposed on children in the family because the parents need to vent their frustration and anger over being unemployed, stuck in a bad marriage, or poor.

Roles in unhealthy families can impose terrible damage on a child's spirit, leaving scars that last a lifetime.

9. In fully-functioning families, the general atmosphere is one of fun and spontaneity.

Healthy families are made up of people of all ages who are unafraid to interact with one another, able to tease and be teased in an attitude of fun, and without feelings being hurt.

Good families can say and do what feels right at the time. They don't worry excessively that someone will take their words or actions the wrong way and be hurt or become angry with them. Of course there are rules of politeness and concern for the feelings of others, but this concern does not become a paranoid fear as happens in unhealthy families.

Jean Piaget, the famous Swiss child psychologist, said that play is the work of children. He couldn't have been more correct. Without play, a child's world is fearful, dark, and boring.

Parents who see the world through fear-darkened glasses, even though they may be Christian, can be expected to turn their children into fearful people unable to experience the joy of the Lord and unwilling to trust themselves to have fun.

10. In healthy families, mistakes are forgiven and used as teaching tools.

Do Christian parents really expect that their children will grow up in this sinful world without any problems, mistakes, or failures? When a mistake occurs in a child or teenager, it must be dealt with with appropriate discipline. But the discipline will be covered with grace and love, just as the discipline God sends our way, called chastening, is laced with grace and love.

In healthy, fully-functioning Christian families, misbehavior is seen as correctable and not necessarily as a basic part of the child's character. Some forms of misbehavior are sin, but not all. If the misbehavior is sin-based, such as disobedience, then the child will be dealt with both from a parental perspective and from a spiritual perspective.

If, however, the child's behavior is a manifestation of a normal aspect of development, such as refusing to share a toy with a playmate at age four, then the wise and careful Christian parent will downplay the sin aspect of the action and simply teach the child how to behave without trying to convince him that he has offended almighty God with his four-year-old behavior.

No one reading this book needs convincing that sin is a basic part of our nature as human beings. Careful parents will be quick to forgive their children, and use that event as a tool to teach the love and forgiveness of God.

11. *The final characteristic of the fully-functioning Christian family relates to the nature of the family unit itself.*

Though mentioned earlier, the function of the family is so important that I cannot close this section without emphasizing a most significant point.

Simply stated, the family exists for the individuals, not the reverse. This seems like such an obvious truth, but so often, failure to observe it lies at the heart of dysfunctional Christian families.

God created the family for the purpose of birthing, rearing, and releasing children. This is evidenced with the first family, Adam and Eve, and continues to this day. Children, therefore, do not exist to support the family unit, sustain it's history, or honor the family name. If these things can be accomplished, fine. But these are not reasons for channeling a growing child's life in a certain direction. Family loyalty is not an important biblical concept.

Obedience to parents, honoring of parents, caring for parents, yes. But surrendering God's leading to the wishes of parents, no. Over and over again we see Jesus telling those who would be his followers to leave their family and come with him. "Let the dead bury the dead," would sound harsh and uncaring if the words were not those of the Savior. First things first, Jesus seems to be saying. Set your family business, loyalties, and commitments aside and do the work of your heavenly Father.

Healthy, fully functioning Christian families understand that God has ordained their family to raise and release children and glorify Him in so doing. They understand the family serves its members, and not the reverse.

Where are you?

If Bill and Aletha Carswell remind you of yourself or your spouse, are you prepared to deal with it before the kind of damage they experienced visits your home?

Is it possible that the lessons the Carswell children learned from their parents could be learned from you? Could you be teaching harmful lessons to your children without knowing it? If so, are you prepared to make the needed corrections?

High-Risk Kids

The writer of Proverbs reminds parents to "Train a child in the way he should go, and, when he is old he will not turn from it" (Proverbs 22:6). Both an encouragement and a warning, this passage and many others emphasize the power of early experiences on the ultimate development of every human being.

The Bible is well-supplied with examples of grown children gone bad. Missing however, are the specific reasons for their sinful and rebellious behavior.

Were David's sons Absalom and Adonijah the victims of neglect or abuse? Were the sons of Eli, described as "worthless men," that way because of their own sinful behavior or because of some secret sin in the family?

Were the writers of Holy Scripture speaking generally about some "bad" children or did they have an individual child in mind?

Were the following passages aimed at someone in particular? "If a man curses his father or mother, his lamp will be snuffed out in pitch darkness" (Proverbs 20:20); or "People will oppress each other—man against man, neighbor against neighbor. The young will rise up against the old, the base against the honorable"(Isaiah 3:5).

We don't know if God had particular people in mind, but we do know that the emphasis in God's Word is on the long-term development of rebellion, toughness, conceit, disobedience, and general arrogance in young people.

What happens, gets started early and lasts, in most cases, a lifetime. In attempting to understand "tough kids" in Christian families, we must recognize two principles.

The first is that God has no grandchildren. Every person at any age beyond the earliest years must decide for him- or herself to walk with or away from the Savior. Nearly perfect Christian parents can have a totally rebellious and unrepentant child, teenager, or adult. It's unlikely, yes, but not impossible. The unique combination of the sin nature and free will work together to ensure that we are not puppets, but free agents making our own choices before God. Parents will answer to God for their parenting practices, but the individual person will not be allowed to blame their sin on any one but themselves.

The second point is that there are no guarantees in the Bible, no assurances that any parental act will produce a certain response in a child. We are called upon to do our best in a very sinful world. We parents are burdened with the same sin-limited brain as everyone else. We should not expect to engage in error-free parenting, nor should we expect to be able to understand all that is happening in our family.

We are limited. But thank God, we also have the guidance and leadership of the Holy Spirit and the revelation of the Bible. Some kids become tough because they have experienced bad parenting. Others become tough simply because they want to. The first group is a reflection of the emphasis God places on the family and early experiences, the second is a reflection of the basic nature of all human beings. As we begin this examination of the high-risk kid, we acknowledge that much is unknown.

But here is what we do know!

The Earliest Days

Infants cannot be "tough," in the sense of the term as we are applying it. Babies are born innocent of individual sin and are not held liable for individual sin until they are of an "age of accountability" known only to God. But this does not negate the great importance of very early experience on the eventual development of a life.

The reality of a difficult labor and delivery on future behavior problems is well-recognized. Any difficulty during pregnancy that causes negative stress can impact the unborn child. Many pediatricians and obstetricians believe unusual anxiety in a pregnant woman can be related to hyperactivity and irritability later on. Extreme upset during pregnancy can result in physical problems, such as harelip and other disfigurements like a cleft palate.

Infants can be placed at high risk because of a genetic predisposition to mental illness. Prebirth trauma such as the mother's being addicted to alcohol or drugs can create problems later on. Other difficulties which can impact the development of a child include if the mother is emotionally disturbed; prematurity and low birth weight; difficult labor and delivery, including medical complications; being separated from the mother soon after birth; and any other disruption in the care provided the infant.

Divorce, incarceration, illness, military deployment, even day care can lead to the eventual breaking of the attachment bond between parent and child leading to an eventual classification of "toughness."

What should a parent look for in babies less than one year old?

High-risk signs

Infants who appear excessively passive or lifeless, or who do not seem to be paying any attention to their surroundings are reason for concern. Causes of this uninvolvement can be physical, including hearing disorders. But the more basic and troubling cause of extreme passivity is psychological.

The baby appears to feel as if something were wrong, and may even look worried and fearful. This is especially troubling and worrisome if the infant interacts this way with parents and siblings. Another sign of high risk is poor eye contact. It is significant when an infant seems uncomfortable making eye-to-eye contact with people well-known to him or her. Some children in this category will actively resist, even fight, getting too close to someone's face. They act almost as if they were frightened of that person.

Babies are expected to cry with conviction, letting the message out they need something, and they need it "now"! Those who are characterized by weak cries, or by more or less constant whining, are cause for concern. Along with crying, a normal infant will seek close physical contact and will want to be picked up and hugged. An infant who does not seem to desire this or who actively fights attempts by others to hug and cuddle should be evaluated by a child development specialist.

The key to this category for the parent is interpersonal behavior between the infant and any other person. This is especially obvious when the child, in addition to refusing to make eye contact, also will not smile. This absence of smiling behavior indicates several possibilities, none of them good. The child could be mentally dysfunctional or autistic, and the failure to smile a result of that.

Or the child is unwilling to "give in" to the invitation to interact, for reasons unknown. Thus, babies who do not make eye contact, will not be held, hugged, or cuddled, do not smile, are passive and lethargic, cry weakly or whine a great deal, and do not seem to favor their mother over other people are giving out warning signals that something is wrong. Left undiagnosed and untreated, babies expressing these symptoms are very likely to be found in the "high-risk" category later on.

Toddlers to teens

We are examining a considerable time period when we consider kids between the years of three and twenty, but the time frame is not as important as the behavioral and attitudinal characteristics of tough kids. During these years kids move from the family into the school environment, out of the home and into the neighborhood, and away from people who must like them to people who can "take them or leave them."

The world of other kids is extremely important. We all learn to evaluate ourselves as we play and attend school with others of our age group. We learn to identify our strengths and weaknesses. We learn how to behave based on what we see others do and what we experience as we try to do those things too. Family is very important in this process of course, but family cannot do a complete job alone. We must face others who do not feel required to treat us in any particular way and learn from the interaction.

As important as school and neighborhood is to the child's own sense of self, parents also rely on others to help them understand their child. Parents must be able to see their child playing and interacting with others of the same age group in order to more accurately evaluate their child. Some may be uncomfortable with the idea of parents evaluating their children, but let me suggest that this is one of the most critical responsibilities facing parents. How else would we be able to know that our children are less mature than expected for their age? How else can we see if our children are shy or assertive with others except that they spend time with others?

And for our discussion in this chapter, how else can parents know when something is wrong with their child's interpersonal behavior except by observing that child in the company of other kids?

Children of any age beyond infancy will test their limits. This is a part of growing up and is not a cause for concern—as long as the "testing" is within a normal range. As a family therapist, I am much more concerned with a child or teen who does no testing of his or her limits, compared to a child or teen who tests often and with determination.

Warning Signs

Testing limits is a part of the process, but tough kids go far beyond "normal" testing. They do not seem to learn needed lessons from their experiences with discipline. The equation should read CTD = L (Child x Testing x Discipline = Learning), and for most kids it does!

But for tough kids, the equation does not work. For tough kids, the equation often reads CTD = R (repetition) instead of L(learning). Why tough kids have trouble learning from their experiences is the big question. It's one that can be only partially answered. Sometimes we can discover the causes through family counseling or therapy, but usually we are unable to find the answer, or we must be satisfied with an incomplete answer.

If answers to the problems experienced with tough kids are to be found, it will take the combined efforts of parents and family therapist over many sessions. *Beware of pat answers!* There are no shortcuts to solving problems with tough kids.

Extreme Resistance

Probably the hallmark of tough kids at any age is extreme and untypical resistance to controls of any kind. This resistance will include talking back to parents and other adults, whining when forced to comply, temper outbursts, and constant arguing over even the smallest point of disagreement.

The tough kid will not only disobey, but also attempt to undermine the authority of the adult in charge. The tough kid will complain that no one has the "right" to tell him or her what to do. Forced compliance will be accompanied with screams of "It's not fair! It's not fair!"

In an adolescent, resistance will be more sophisticated and thought-out and will involve more attempts at manipulation than outright disobedience. This may include trying to play one parent against the other, trying to get the school counselor to be on their side when the assistant principal has already made a disciplinary decision, or begging for just one more chance to prove how repentant they really have become. Tough teenagers do not believe anyone has the "right" to tell them what they can or cannot do.

Note that this can happen in families where the child has been adequately disciplined all his or her young life. Toughness does not have to be the result of poor parenting!

Cruelty

The tough child can be expected to be cruel to pets and smaller children, and may even show a tendency to hurt himself. Many kids in this category will try to tattoo themselves, even though this is very painful. The tough kid will be observed pulling a wing off a fly just to see what will happen, or pinching a puppy to see how long it will take until it cries. The list is endless and very discouraging. But note that these behaviors are not common to more normal kids, and indicate a problem of some seriousness.

As teenagers, the tough kids will express cruelty by even more tattoos and body marks, and will gravitate to death, pain, and gore as themes of movies and music. T-shirts will be black and contain violent or antisocial messages. Drinking and drug use are very common, and are a part of the antisocial mind-set of the tough teen. "No one can tell me what to do," wails the tough teen, and this theme is reinforced by music, movies, and friends. Describing the companions of the tough teen as "friends" is not usually accurate.

The tough teen will have many "acquaintances" but few, if any, true friends. Tough kids are loners who hang out with other loners. No one is trusted as a friend, and anyone is open to being exploited by those who are stronger. Tough teens will not acknowledge their feelings, believing that doing so is a sign of weakness. Fighting is common, and scars are a sign of courage.

All authority figures are rejected. Even sports heroes and music idols are rejected as having "sold out."

The cruelty that is so typical of the tough kid is experienced by family members too. The more painful stories of my counseling experiences come from the parents of tough teens who could not understand how their "child" could want to hurt them so much.

This is usually not an unfair description of what has been happening at home. The tough kid is so angry and defiant that the family is not spared his or her wrath. The most vile and obscene language is used in arguing with parents. The cruelest kind of comments are directed at mom and dad, even siblings, all with apparent intent to hurt.

Callous Independence

Every wise parent wants children who will grow to be independent adults, able to care for themselves and not needing to rely on others for their basic needs. Tough kids are independent too, but it is a callous, defiant independence unrelated to true maturity. The tough kid as a child will not become upset when dropped off at the day care center or church nursery. He or she will not cry as a toddler when mom leaves the room as other children do, acting almost as if they didn't care. *They don't!*

The independence we see in tough kids does not have maturity as it's goal, but rebellion and manipulation. Tough kids in this extreme category can be expected to win over people they meet casually, often appearing smooth and self-confident when in reality their feelings are limited to simply not caring what the other person thinks of them.

As younger children, tough kids often have trouble making eye contact. Later on, as teenagers, this requires constant wearing of sunglasses for guys and very heavy eye makeup for girls. Also missing are smiles! One of the more striking comments from people who are with tough kids on a regular basis is how rarely they smile. We know smiling is an intensely interpersonal event for people generally, and it seems to be this interpersonal quality that turns tough kids off to smiling. They do not seem to want to admit that they are having fun or building a relationship with another person.

Instead, they choose to think of themselves as superior, independent, and too "cool" to have fun.

As older teens and young adults, this callous independence means that intimate relationships will be of the one-night stand variety rather than a sustained relationship or marriage. Males will appear as "con men" and women as "seductive." Their adult lives will be filled with unhappy and unsuccessful relationships and poor work histories. They will be difficult to get to know because they seem to lack a clear idea of who they are. This results in the need to dress and act a certain role. Manifestly unhappy, they will turn to alcohol or drugs to feel better about themselves.

Regressive tendencies

As younger children, tough kids will act immature for their age. Bed-wetting will continue far longer than is normal. Bottles and diapers may be clung to into the fourth year or longer. Though callously independent, they may cling to objects as security symbols rather than people. These regressive tendencies are compounded by impulsiveness. Tough kids need to get what they want immediately or extreme upset will result. Continuing into adolescence and adulthood, the tough kid may be a compulsive overeater, chain-smoker, or nail-biter. Sexually out of control in most cases, there will be a pattern of promiscuity, unwanted pregnancies, sexually transmitted diseases, abortions, and failed marriages. The tough kid as an adult is still a "kid" in an adult's body, with all the compulsiveness and lack of personal discipline we would expect from a small child. When others describe this person as an adolescent or adult, they use terms such as "acts like a little kid when he doesn't get what he wants" and "you just never know what will set her off."

105

Accident proneness

One of the more difficult to explain manifestations of toughness is constant accidents and mishaps. As small children, there will be a constant need for bandages and visits to the doctor. Broken bones, bruises, burned fingers, cuts and scratches all are common to these children. It is not uncommon for their parents to be suspected of child abuse because of this. As adolescents and young adults, there will be a string of automobile accidents, and car insurance will be nearly impossible to obtain. They will always, it seems, have an arm in a soft cast or a finger in a splint. There will be numerous scars to brag about and their ability to "take" the pain will always be mentioned. Husbands, wives, and parents will become quickly fed up with their constant breaking of things, losing jobs because of accidents at work coupled with a professed inability to get another job because of being "injured" previously. The reasons for accident proneness seems to be a combination of poor self-concept, leading to hesitation and poor judgement and a desire to manipulate and control others through their injuries.

"Leave him alone" one mother told me about her teenage son. "If we hassle him about his drinking, he will just have another car wreck." A lifetime pattern, accident proneness should not be overlooked or written off as mere "clumsiness."

Immoral/amoral

All small children are amoral, in the sense that they have not yet learned the rules by which their group lives nor how to conform to those standards. Amorality only applies to children of such a young age that they are unaware of what is expected of them. To describe a person as immoral implies an ability to understand, coupled with an opportunity to know the expectation.

106

Semi-tough, tough, and super-tough kids all begin life as amoral creations. Many of the tough, and most if not all of the super-tough kids, go on into adolescence and adulthood being immoral. They never break free of this limitation. To enable parents and others to correctly diagnose and understand the problem they may be facing, it is necessary to say what many do not wish to hear: some of these tough kids will not be reached by conventional means, and some will not be reached at all.

Kids in this category lie habitually, steal with no reason, blame others when caught, protest their innocence in the face of overwhelming evidence to the contrary, and do not seem to feel any guilt or remorse when confronted.

Is this what Jesus was describing in Matthew 13:14-15? "In them is fulfilled the prophecy of Isaiah: 'You will be ever hearing but never understanding; you will be ever seeing but never perceiving. For this people's ear has become calloused; they hardly hear with their ears, and they have closed their eyes. Otherwise they might see with their eyes, hear with their ears, understand with their hearts and turn, and I would heal them.' "

Sandy

Sandy, 34, sits on death row in a Virginia prison, convicted of killing his wife and attempting to kill her parents. Sandy has been in prison for nearly five years. He has not seen his two sons during that time, and no longer asks to see them.

Sandy grew up in a Christian family in Richmond, Virginia. He attended a Christian school in the area, graduated, and enrolled in a Christian college. There he met the girl who would later be his wife. Sandy was a high "B" student in college and was elected president of his class in both his sophomore and junior years. Sandy was a "preacher boy," the label given to young men who felt called to preach and were in training for ministry. Universally well thought of, Sandy gave no indication of the horror that would happen in only a few years.

Sandy was moral in every sense; he had no history of law-breaking or extreme rebelliousness as a child, holding a good Christian testimony and reputation. This middle-class young man was set to explode, but his fuse smoldered in secret. No one knew.

The crisis came five years after his graduation. For four of those years, Sandy had been the senior pastor of a mid-size, Bible-believing, church in Virginia.

Then one Saturday afternoon, the 28-year-old pastor took his wife out on a boat ride and murdered her. Her body was recovered weeks afterward. Had the anchor chain that was wrapped around her body not slipped off, Sandy might still be free.

Convinced that a confession might spare him of the death penalty, Sandy slowly confessed the unbelievable story of what had led up to the murder. He had been planning it for at least two years, believing that his wife was planning to leave him.

Sandy's wife had apparently been told that her husband was not only having several "affairs" with women in the church but had also threatened one of them with violence if she revealed what had been going on.

Becoming increasingly frightened, she had written a letter to a friend telling about a possible divorce, only to have Sandy read the return letter from the friend. Thus, the murder of this young wife and mother by her professing Christian husband took place. The investigation that was required by the trial uncovered even more disturbing facts.

Sandy actually *had* been in a great deal of trouble as a teenager, but he had always been "bailed out" by his business man/deacon father who was worried that scandal would hurt him financially.

At one point, a large donation to the church connected to the Christian high school Sandy attended resulted in his record being "cleared" so that the Christian college he wanted to attend would accept him.

In college, Sandy's roommates suspected him to be a phony, but his social skills were so polished that he was able to run for class president and win in two succeeding years. Teachers thought well of him and were happy to recommend him for the associate pastorate position that led to his senior pastorate at age 24.

Sandy's dynamic speaking ability and social graces got him quickly approved by the congregation. This was all the more reason for the church to refuse to believe the rumors of sexual misbehavior that were beginning to surface.

Sandy had serious problems as early as second grade that always seemed to involve dishonesty of some type. They involved stealing lunch money, lying without apparent reason, and fighting—but he was always successful in blaming the other kid involved. When all else failed, dad would get him out of trouble, thus preserving a "clean" record.

Sandy was a sociopath in Christian clothing, a con artist who chose the field of religion to practice his carefully crafted deceptions and lies. Sandy had fooled the system and hundreds, maybe thousands, of people into believing he was something he was not. And he had started the deceptions as a little child.

Sandy will probably die for his deceptions. He will protest to the end that it was not really his fault.

Andrew

Andrew was a tough kid, too. Bad family background. Bad neighborhood. Bad parents. Bad schools. Bad everything! But today Andrew is not in prison, and never has been. He is the father of three children and the husband of one wife. He and his family attend church regularly, and minister to others. He is active in community matters and will likely one day run for political office.

Andrew is as much a success as Sandy is a failure.

Andrew arose from the ashes of a terrible childhood and has a proven track record of success both as a Christian and as a citizen. He had abusive and neglectful parents, but he does neither to his children. He saw his father beat his mother on a regular basis but has never come close to striking his wife. His father was an alcoholic but Andrew does not drink or do drugs. His parents never saw the inside of any church building, but Andrew's family never misses church.

Can such opposites as Sandy and Andrew be explained?

Probably not to everyone's satisfaction, but we can note that Sandy was a polished liar at an early age who professed Jesus Christ as personal Savior as a part of his con job on people. Andrew was confronted with the reality of his need for forgiveness as a young man, was turned to Jesus Christ and found Him true to His word.

What was most strikingly different for these two men went far beyond their vastly different income levels and social class. What worked for one and not the other was the saving power of Jesus Christ—spurned by Sandy and embraced by Andrew.

Sandy did not choose, at least as of right now, to trust Jesus to redeem him from his miserable condition.

Andrew did!

What worked for one and not the other was salvation. Of

course salvation could work for Sandy too, but he doesn't seem close to that right now.

Do these stories tell what to expect from our own growing children? Perhaps. But more than that, we need to be reminded again and again that we are not in complete charge of these "loaners" from God. The weaknesses and sinful tendencies we see in our youngsters may or may not be the fault of their parents. (Experience tells us that "probably not" is usually closer to the truth.)

As we continue to study and discuss high-risk kids and high-risk families, then, we need to realize that blame for the behavior of tough kids cannot automatically be laid at the door of their parents. This should encourage us as we examine our children's behavior in the following quiz.

Quiz For Worried Parents

Answer the following questions yes or no.

_____1. Has your child stolen without confronting the victim? This includes forgery.

_____2. Has your child run away from home overnight at least twice?

_____3. Does your child often lie without reason?

_____4. Has your child deliberately set fires in dangerous locations?

_____5. Is your child often truant from school?

_____6. Has your child broken into someone's house, building, or car?

_____7. Has your child deliberately destroyed the property of others?

_____8. Has your child been physically cruel to animals?

_____9. Has your child forced someone into sexual activity with him or her?

____10. Has your child used a weapon in a fight?

____11. Does your child often start physical fights?

____12. Has your child ever stolen directly from the victim, as in a face-to-face confrontation?

____13. Has your child ever been physically cruel to people of any age?

Mom and dad, three or more "yes" answers indicates that you may have a major problem on your hands. Diagnosis and intervention by trained professionals is in order. Answers in the affirmative on these questions indicates that you may have a "super-tough" kid on your hands, and should not delay in getting that child or young person some help.

But if these questions describe more serious experiences than you have faced, try the next set to see if you have a less serious problem on your hands.

____1. Does your child often lose his or her temper?

____2. Does your child often argue with you and other adults?

____3. Does your child actively defy or refuse adult requests or rules such as curfew or chores at home?

____4. Does your child deliberately do things that annoy other people?

____5. Does your child often blame others for his or her own mistakes?

____6. Is your child often touchy or easily annoyed by others?

____7. Is your child often angry and resentful?

____8. Is your child often spiteful or vindictive?

____9. Does your child often swear or use obscene language?

If you answered "yes" at least five times, and the problem asked about has been in your home for at least six months, you may have a "tough" kid to deal with.

It's less serious, but still nothing to fool around with. This kid needs counseling, and his or her parents probably need support. While tough kids are less difficult to deal with than super-tough kids, problems left unresolved can grow into something much worse. Parents facing a crisis with a child, teen, or young adult outlined in one of the two categories just mentioned need to act now.

If they describe your child, you should contact a school counselor, ask for an appointment at a local child guidance clinic or mental health center, contact a private counseling agency, talk with a person on the church staff who is trained to know how to deal with such matters, or call your family physician for a referral.

But the key is to act, not to wait. Take a proactive rather than reactive stance in dealing with the problem.

Too many parents try to hide the truth from themselves, as though it was somehow their responsibility that they were trusted to raise a tough kid. These kids do not belong to us, nor does their behavior reflect on us—unless we want it to.

But what will reflect on you as parents is your refusal to recognize and deal with a difficult problem while the child is of an age when intervention will help.

Tough kids who can't help it

Raising a hyperactive, attention-deficit child is tough enough. But when parents hold conservative religious beliefs that emphasize the cardinal importance of well-behaved children, the challenges to parent and child multiply greatly.

Linda and I raised such a child, and we know a little of what many parents experience. Self-doubt haunts parents of tough kids.

We have questions about discipline. We worry about being accused of child abuse because we become angry when discipline does not work. And we question why God delivered such a challenging "tough" child into our care in the first place.

Hyperactivity is one of the major "involuntary" problems we will discuss in this chapter. We will also examine learning disorders and try to explain the impact of these "school-based" conditions on the family. In addition, we'll make some suggestions designed to help child, parents, and the whole family.

Trevor

Linda and I became Christians in the early sixties, and quickly got involved in a "young marrieds" Sunday School class in a solid, Bible-preaching church in the Detroit area. This experience not only brought us into close contact with good Bible teaching and preaching, but with numbers of other recently married Christian couples as well. Linda and I were connected with this one adult class for nearly fourteen years, and we developed close friendships with couples who shared their child-rearing challenges and frustrations with us.

Trevor is the first child of Bonnie and Lewis Young. Bonnie did not work outside the home when Trevor was young, and Lewis was a supervisor in a large paper factory in Detroit. Committed Christians, dedicated to serving in the local church, this couple was convinced that God was going to raise up either a president of the United States or the world's greatest preacher out of their family.

Then they began to notice some behaviors in Trevor that suggested that maybe this child was not going to be the one to fulfill their family dream.

By the time Trevor was four, he had exhibited a range of behaviors that convinced everyone familiar with the child that something was wrong. Trevor took someone's lunch money when he was in kindergarten. He went into the teacher's desk to get the bathroom pass when he was not given permission quickly enough. He "borrowed" another child's wristwatch in the second grade, then lied when asked about it.

The pattern continued into high school. Although medicine helped, what seemed to be the final answer was puberty— that time of life when we go through major hormonal and metabolic changes connected with sexual maturity.

The experts don't have a clear explanation for why so many

115

hyperactive kids get better during their teen years, but most seem to.

As a youngster, Trevor did not seem to need as much sleep as other children. When he became tired, however, he would go to sleep almost no matter where he was, then wake up suddenly, almost on the run. Trevor seemed unable to keep his hands from touching things and he appeared uncontrollably curious about *everything!* He would ask a million questions but never wait for a complete answer.

He was excessively distractible and had great difficulty finishing his schoolwork. Homework seemed an impossible task—his parents once mentioned that the only way to get their son to finish his work would be to seal him into a 55-gallon drum so he would not be distracted by what was going on around him.

Trevor was, therefore, criticized and disciplined by nearly all his teachers. By the time his problem began to diminish, he had developed quite a reputation as an uncontrollable child

Do you have a Trevor?

We did! Our Trevor was named Laurie. To determine if your "tough kid" could be hyperactive and attention-deficit disordered, ask yourself the following questions.

_____ 1. Have we and other adults (school teachers, babysitters, Sunday School teachers, etc., complained about this child's inattentiveness, impulsivity, and restlessness on a regular basis?

_____ 2. Was this child younger than six before these problems began?

_____ 3. Is this child significantly more restless, etc., compared to others of his or her age?

_____ 4. Has the child exhibited these bothersome

behaviors for at least twelve months?

_____ 5. Is the child free of other conditions (retardation, physical handicap) that could account for the extremes in behavior?

_____ 6. Is your answer "yes" to at least ten of the following statements about your child?

Activity/Rating Scale

_____ 1. When playing, does your child talk too much?

_____ 2. Does your child seem to sleep less than other children?

_____ 3. Does your child have unusual difficulty getting to sleep?

_____ 4. When watching television, does your child get up and down often?

_____ 5. Does your child often interrupt others when they are trying to watch television?

_____ 6. When watching television, does your child also play with other objects or toys?

_____ 7. Is your child unable to play quietly?

_____ 8. Is your child restless or disruptive when visiting relatives?

_____ 9. Is your child restless or in a hurry when shopping?

_____ 10. When playing, does your child constantly move from one toy or activity to another?

_____ 11. At mealtime, does your child get up, move about, or do other things?

_____ 12. At mealtime, does your child interrupt others without seeming to notice that they are doing so?

_____ 13. At playtime, does your child constantly try to get the attention of adults?

_____ 14. Does your child talk too much during playtime?

_____15. Is your child unusually restless at church or at the movies?

_____16. Is your child restless and fidgety during travel?

_____17. Is your child restless during sleep?

_____18. During meals, does your child talk too much?

_____19. When watching television, does your child wiggle?

_____20. Does your child seem to break toys often?

If you have answered "yes" to at least half of these twenty questions, you may have a hyperactive, attention-deficit child on your hands. If so, you are certainly not alone. *Approximately five percent of elementary age children fit into this category.*

A word to parents

Our first child was hyperactive. *Was!* The vast majority of hyperactive children have been released from this condition by the time they become young adolescents, and you can expect this to be true in your family too.

But it is important to note that a proper diagnosis is critical. No book, no matter how thorough, could come close to the accuracy of the family physician or the child's pediatrician.

Linda and I were both relieved and helped when our child was confirmed as being hyperactive. Now we knew what we were dealing with, and we knew that most of what our daughter did that became problems for us were not conscious decisions to do wrong, but rather the result of impulsivity and distractibility that were largely beyond her control.

We were not bad parents and Laurie was not a bad child!

We were good parents struggling as hard as we knew how to deal with a problem neither of us had ever faced before. We were getting help, and fortunately, Laurie was in the seventy-five percent of hyperactive kids who are helped with medicine. And we were reminded that if we remained strong, Laurie would probably grow out of her hyperactivity in a few years. *Years!*

Sure enough, the doctor's words proved true. Yes, the years were tough, but not beyond our ability to manage. The same will prove true in your family.

But let's be honest. Until the child grows out of hyperactivity, challenges will be omnipresent. I offer the following description of the typical hyperactive child in hopes that careful consideration by parents and other adults will help us to correctly diagnose the problems our children may present to us so that we will be able to get them the help needed while maintaining our own sanity as parents.

The kids will survive hyperactivity, but sometimes we wonder about their parents.

Specific Problems of Hyperactive Children

Behavior: These "tough kids" exhibit a short attention span, are very distractible, usually restless, have poor impulse control, and tend to be both destructive and noisy. In other words, hyperactive kids present themselves to the world as "pests."

They're the kind of kids who are always in your face, asking questions but not waiting for an answer, asking what they can do, complaining about being bored while surrounded with toys and games, cranky because of insufficient sleep but unwilling to take a nap or go to bed on time.

They're always breaking things, but then sincerely apologizing that "I didn't mean do it"—which is probably more true than false, and they're *loud!*

119

Anyone who cares for children will know within 15 minutes if there is a hyperactive child in the group.

We love these kids, because they truly do not mean to create such problems for themselves and others. And they feel both guilty and confused when they misbehave. But their guilt will not prevent them from repeating their impulsive misdeeds. This repetition produces even more confusion and guilt, and if we are not careful, we can have a full-blown anxious, self-destructive kid on our hands by age six or seven.

Parents must know how to deal with this condition in order to control the damage that is almost inevitable. Inevitable damage? Yes. Just ask the grown-ups who used to be hyperactive and you will see the damage. But it can be *minimized*.

Social Activities: Hyperactive kids have a history of problems with peers. The behaviors that go along with hyperactivity irritate children as well as adults. Even other hyperactive kids don't want to be around hyperactive kids!

Hyperactive children are regarded as disobedient and disrespectful to adults. While true, this is as much the result of not listening and of being distracted as it is a matter of willful disobedience. This relates to social development, because children, as a rule, resent kids who are always causing trouble in the school or group.

Add to this the aggressive play patterns common to hyperactivity, coupled with lying and stealing caused by their impulsivity, and you have a kid no one wants to play with. Hyperactive kids have a tendency to engage in high-risk activities and are therefore "scary" to many of the other kids and their parents.

Show me a hyperactive child and I'll show you a child with scars. These kids are always getting hurt, and their parents are in danger of being falsely accused of child abuse. The general social package of the hyperactive child is not a good one. A strong family can make up for some of the social problems, but only some of them. Hyperactive kids will remember their childhood as being lonely and filled with getting into trouble.

Thinking Patterns: We already know that a hyperactive child suffers from inattention and distractibility. These two conditions tend to smother all others in terms of importance. If the child were not afflicted with these two, he or she simply would not be diagnosed as hyperactive in the first place. But beyond inattention and distractibility, we find problems in developing a proper conscience. Because of constantly "getting into trouble" even at a very young age, hyperactive kids struggle to know what is right and wrong. They are confused (to say nothing of their parents!) about why they keep getting into trouble when they really don't mean to do anything wrong.

"What's wrong with me?" they ask. "I know what is right and what will make adults happy, but I seem unable to behave that way on a regular basis."

We Christian parents have a real challenge here, because our hyperactive kids are attending the same Sunday School classes as other, better-behaved children who get rewarded for their "good" behavior. The hyperactive child who wants to be "good" just cannot seem to behave that well!

Impulsivity carries with it the failure to adequately learn about the relationship between present behavior and future consequences. This leads to risk-taking behavior and a failure to learn from past mistakes. That cause-effect displacement is a key concern in helping hyperactive kids survive their tough years and be able to do well once the hyperactivity has passed from the scene.

Academic Performance: It will come as no surprise to anyone reading this material that hyperactive kids do not do well in school. They tend to be classified as "underachieving for intelligence." This means that they possess the intelligence to perform, but do not manifest that intelligence on test scores or assignments.

It is also worrisome that hyperactivity seems to carry with it a tendency to develop learning disabilities. We will examine learning disabilities in detail later in this chapter, but for now we can just accept that a hyperactive child is going to perform in school well below expectations and ability.

Emotional Functioning: Hyperactive kids are not happy kids. No person, child or adult, would be happy with the failure and problem rate common to hyperactive kids. Consequently, these kids tend to experience bouts of depression characterized by loss of appetite, sleep disorders, self-assurance habits such as thumb-sucking or masturbation, and a general attitude and appearance of having given up on attempts to improve their situation. Low self-esteem is to be expected due to school performance problems and getting into trouble at home.

Hyperactive kids tend to express immature emotional functioning across the board, are easily angered and frustrated, easily excited, and confused about the situation they seem unable to change. The typical hyperactive kid is often happy and excited—then quickly unhappy, angry and depressed. Up and down, up and down, the pattern will probably continue until puberty.

Physical Characteristics: One of the most perplexing qualities of hyperactivity is the connection to physical traits, including being small for one's age, experiencing immature bone

122

growth, frequent upper respiratory infections, a tendency to be allergic to many things, unusual physical characteristics (including inward pointing "pinky" fingers on both hands, third toe being longer than the second, "electric" hair that seems to point in all directions, unusual "swirls" of hair, ears lower and out of line, and a deeply furrowed tongue).

Other physical traits include short sleep cycles, high pain tolerance, and poor coordination. How these physical characteristics relate to hyperactivity is unknown at this point, but the frequency with which they are found in these children has led to much research.

In conclusion, let me offer a word on causation.

Hyperactivity is a term that includes a range of physical, academic, cognitive, and social difficulties none of which are the child's fault.

There are multiple suspected causes, the most widely accepted of which are hereditary factors and birth complications.

Toxic agents such as lead ingestion through eating lead-based paint chips, or carbon monoxide poisoning, also lead to this condition.

It is significant for parents to realize how helpless the child is when it comes to correcting this problem behavior. It will take all our energy as parents, combined with good professional intervention, if we are going to meet the developmental needs of this tough kid. But it can be done.

Linda and I did it, as did countless other parents of hyperactive kids. The challenge will strain your spirituality and your marriage. It will make you wonder what you did to deserve such a needy child. But the job *can* be done.

Parents of children suspected of being hyperactive need to get a professional evaluation as soon as possible, and begin treatment and home-based corrections as soon as possible.

Some of the disciplinary recommendations for use with all children, including those that are hyperactive, will be discussed in a later chapter.

For now, we will turn to a second very common tough kid, the learning disabled child.

Learning Problems

Perhaps one child in a hundred has never had problems in his or her studies, in taking tests, getting homework done on time, and other school-based behaviors. Some kids are very bright and well motivated, and many do well in school. But most of us can remember a time when we "failed" at something in school. We can remember what it felt like when that phone call came and we just knew it was the teacher asking to meet with our parents. We remember because it was probably an isolated event, once a semester or so, and we responded by "shaping up" and keeping mom and dad, and the teacher, off our collective cases.

But I could introduce you to dozens of people for whom this scenario was a daily or weekly event—kids for whom having problems in school was as natural as eating breakfast—and just about as expected. For kids like these, doing well was the unusual event, doing badly the norm!

I am describing learning disabled kids, another category of involuntary tough kids. These children have no choice but to struggle with their studies; they have almost no chance of getting the teacher's praise or winning awards. Learning disabled kids can do well in school (under the right circumstances and with the correct amount of special help), but most do not get what they need. Consequently, they experience a school career filled with failure and frustration.

Putting on my "family counselor hat" for a moment, I can

testify that parents with learning disabled kids struggle with their own sense of failure as parents almost as much as the "school-tough" kid. Rarely does a parent of an elementary age child enter my office without schoolwork being a part of the problem. As with hyperactivity, the key to helping learning disabled kids is early diagnosis. Knowing that the child's difficulty is not due to laziness or lack of intelligence releases parent and child from the guilt that usually accompanies this condition.

What is a learning disability? Maybe a clarification of terms would be helpful here. A learning disability exists when a child's academic performance falls at least two grades below the average expected for his or her grade and age and does so in at least two subject areas; reading and math, for example.

A true learning disability is considered to be either an inborn trait (this often runs in families), or a result of a birth complication. This would include things such as a difficult labor and delivery, brief oxygen deprivation, and many other medical conditions.

The point is that a true learning disability is totally beyond the child's control, and is not in any way related to motivation, desire to succeed, rebellion, disobedience, etc.

Parents must ask for a diagnosis by a trained professional as soon as differences in performance are noticed. There is very little harm done by testing a child who does not really need it, but tremendous damage done to the child who needs special help but is not tested, and so does not receive special help.

Learning disabilities can be general or specific, impacting every area of learning or just one, such as reading. A learning disability will likely remain in place for life but a child can learn to deal with the condition and avoid developing a pattern of repeated failure. Linda and I have a friend in San

125

Francisco who is a medical doctor specializing in pediatrics and who has been dyslexic *all her life!*

Dyslexia is a condition causing a reversal of letters (in most cases) creating great difficulty in reading. But being bright, and because she was correctly diagnosed early in life, our friend was able to build an impressive academic record and become a medical doctor. A learning disability does not have to be a tragedy.

Parental Reactions

Parents' initial reaction to a diagnosis of learning disability will probably be some form of denial. They will say "He's just stubborn," or "she'll grow out of it" in many different variations. There is a strong tendency to deny the reality of bad news even when the bad news is of a moderate, rather than severe, nature.

Upon reflection, and with the passage of a little time, parents sometimes become angry at the school or teacher who first suggested there could be a learning disability involved in the child's school problems.

The danger is that parents may change schools rather than confront the learning disability. This only delays the start of treatment. It is common for parents to resist the possibility that their child could have an inborn trait that could be life-limiting. They may even express some anger at the child who is disabled, or accuse each other for having this tough kid in the first place.

This powerful anger is often unspoken, but greatly felt by the family members. Parents often have a hard time understanding that the child may have developed some coping strategies, such as a refusal to try new challenges because of past failures. That kind of behavior leads parents

126

to feel that "if he just tried harder, he could overcome this."

When the severity and reality of the learning disability can no longer be denied, and especially when the limitation is diagnosed through testing, parents may once again turn their anger on the school for not noticing it sooner.

Or they may blame themselves for the same "failure." Some even get angry at the child.

Brian

I was in my third year of teaching at Wilson Junior High school when I met Brian. Wilson Junior High was then a 7-8-9th grade junior high of almost 1,100 students. Imagine that many young adolescents in one building all day, five days a week! I worked there for seven years and never had one dull day.

Brian was going to do his best to make sure the "no dull days" record would remain unbroken. I received Brian and the rest of his seventh grade classmates one hot September day, the first day of school. Always an exciting time for kids and school personnel, the opening of school that year would prove to be a time of testing and education for me. Brian and his family would be my teachers.

Brian was an average sized, slightly pudgy, almost thirteen-year-old kid who quickly let his new homeroom and social studies teacher know who was going to be boss. Brian had no intention of doing *anything* any teacher asked him to do, and especially not if it had anything to do with schoolwork. And if that wasn't bad enough, I had to deal with Brian early in the morning during home-room and first-period social studies. Boy, did I need my coffee those mornings! So round and round I went with this twelve year old. He absolutely would *not* participate in any home-room or class activities where he had to do anything of an academic nature. He refused to read aloud when called on. He would *not* respond to challenges to spell words on paper or aloud. Brian was determined to fight it out with me and his other teachers—and so far, no one had conquered him.

Brian was failing virtually every class (he did okay in boys gym and woodshop), and when the six-weeks card marking went home, I enclosed a note asking his parents to come in for a conference. I am sure that parents generally have no idea how much teachers fear and loathe parent-teacher conferences. But as I waited for Brian's mom and dad to come in, I was more apprehensive than any other teacher had ever been.

Only Brian's dad showed up that Thursday evening. A large, pot-bellied man with a stubble beard and alcohol on his breath, Brian's dad looked at me through reddened eyes and asked "What's my kid been up to now?" As we talked, I learned that this family was in the habit of moving from one part of Detroit to another every year or so and Brian had attended at least four different schools by the time he reached me in the seventh grade.

Brian's mother was "sick," his father told me, and would not be coming to any later conferences. This father then proceeded to tell me how Brian had "always" had trouble in school

"Took after his old man, I guess," said his dad, half smiling. "I guess I should tell you that I have tried to get that kid to do his work every way I know. I have threatened him, beat him until he couldn't stand up, warned him that he would be a failure, but nothing ever worked. I guess it is a lost cause, just like his older brothers."

I asked this father if Brian had ever been tested for learning disability, and he said he wasn't sure but he didn't think so.

"We moved around a lot so I guess his other teachers didn't get much of a chance to test him." I asked if they would mind me scheduling some testing for Brian. He answered that it would be okay as long as it didn't cost anything.

Well, I'm sure you can see where I'm going with this. This nasty, mean, bullyish, anti-school twelve-year-old was afflicted with a learning disability that made it virtually impossible for him to be successful at schoolwork under normal circumstances. Brian was diagnosed as having an "Academic Skills Disorder," concentrated in reading and expressive language, with a less severe handicap in arithmetic skills.

Brian couldn't help it! He *couldn't* do his seatwork or homework, no matter how he might have tried when he was younger. It wasn't his fault. Brian was an involuntary tough kid who would only be helped by being moved to a special class for academic subjects where he could get one-on-one help without feeling embarrassed or being a failure.

Brian, I am happy to say, improved markedly by the time he left our school in the ninth grade. I don't think Brian will ever be an astronaut or college professor. His early negative experiences with teachers and school probably limited those possibilities. But he should be okay, and I believe he is.

Do you have a Brian at your house?

We did. Our Brian was named Laurie. Our involuntary tough kid could read well enough but had problems understanding. Our child was hyperactive and could not sit still in school. She acted impulsively rather than out of anger. Laurie got better, with medication and tons of special help from teachers and school psychologists, and most of all, her mother. But it worked!

First, though, comes correct diagnosis. Help starts with testing, and there is always a way to arrange for testing.

Having money helps, but families like Brian's can get the testing they need. That is, if one of us is sharp enough to look beyond the bad behavior and see the kids underneath, who just might be trapped in their misbehavior and totally confused about why they cannot do better, even when they try.

If you think you might know a Brian or a Laurie, or have one in your own family, get them tested so that your "involuntary" tough kid will have a chance in this world.

Jeremiah 1:5 reminds us that God knew us and our children before we knew ourselves. "Before I formed you in the womb" God says, "I knew you...". God neither makes mistakes nor junk. The child delivered into our hands—that hyperactive child who would be such a challenge to a young couple—that child was handed into our care because an all-knowing, all-loving God knew that Linda and I could give Laurie what she needed.

We were selected to be Laurie's parents just as you and countless others were selected to be parents of other tough kids. No mistakes were made! God knew what He was doing when he trusted us with a challenging child, and He is just as careful today.

No mistakes! There are challenges in abundance. Frustrations more than anyone could count. Failures too, for sure! But God knew what He was doing, and we can do nothing more than trust Him and ourselves to do what is best for our children. God doesn't make mistakes!

Bruised Kids, Broken Families:
Abuse and the Tough Kid

The story was unbelievable! But there it was, on the front page of the Greenville, South Carolina, newspaper: "Prominent Greenville businessman and church elder charged with child abuse."

Bob Foreman had been mentioned in the local paper on several previous occasions, but never related to something to be ashamed of. In the past, Bob had always made the paper because of being chosen as outstanding young businessman of the year. Or the business page noted his rapid climb up the corporate ladder of the insurance company where he had been employed since college. Bob had even been mentioned a time or two on the Sunday religion page, recognized for his church leadership and successful fund raising for church causes.

Bob Foreman was a winner in every way, or so it seemed. But a dark cloud had suddenly appeared in his life and threatened every thing he valued. He had just been arrested for physically abusing his eight-year-old son, Barry, and he

131

was going to have to go to trial for what happened. Bob was crushed. He was probably going to lose his position with his company, even if he was found innocent of the charges. His marriage was beginning to crack under the pressure, and his wife had mentioned a need to "get away" for a few days and spend some time with her family. Bob knew that she might never come back.

Equally confused was eight-year-old Barry, who seemed to be somehow the cause of all the terrible things that were happening to his family. Yet all he did was go to school the day after he had gotten a "whipping" from his dad. Barry knew that the spanking (some called it a beating) he received was not unusual. He was always getting into trouble without knowing why.

The incident that brought the problem to the surface began at church one Sunday evening. Barry always had trouble sitting still, and the older he got, the more restless he seemed to become. During the service that Sunday evening, Barry was so fidgety that his dad picked him up and literally carried him out to the church lobby where he was taken by the shoulders and shaken until he thought his head would fly off. (The headache that resulted still hurt when he went to school Monday morning.)

When they arrived home after church, Barry knew his dad was still angry with him for causing a commotion in church. So when Barry spilled his juice on the family room carpet his dad really "lost it." He grabbed Barry and the "licking stick" used for spankings, and proceeded to "spank" his eight-year-old son so severely that the welts were still clearly visible when Barry changed his clothes for gym class Monday afternoon.

Ed Sprague, Barry's gym teacher saw the marks, remembered Barry's complaints of a headache, and called the principal. June Wilkinson, the principal of Barry's school, had been in education long enough to know what the law says about reporting suspected child abuse, and she did not hesitate to call Child Protective Services downtown.

After a visit to the school to examine and talk to Barry, the team made up of a plain-clothes police-woman and a social worker went first to the Foreman home to talk with Barry's mom. When Alice Foreman confirmed that a "spanking" had taken place pretty much as Barry had reluctantly said, they returned to the police department and called Bob Foreman, explained what was taking place, and asked him to come down to the Child Protective Division of the Police Department for an interview. He was firmly told to do so *before* saying anything to his son, and if he could not agree to this requirement, he would be arrested at once. Of course Bob agreed, and left work immediately. Frightened and confused, Bob Foreman went through the interview feeling every bit like the criminal others seemed to assume he was.

Yes, the spanking had taken place. Yes, he probably hit Barry harder and more often that he should, but this kid was always getting into trouble. He just never seemed to learn. Barry could get spanked for doing something and turn right around and do it again a few hours later. Barry was always in trouble at school too, and for this upwardly-mobile, achievement-oriented Christian dad, a son who seemed bound for a life of failure was a heavy burden

What happened? The case did not have to go to public trial. Fortunately, Bob got some good advice from his lawyer and agreed that he had overreacted. He promised not to use physical methods on Barry again, and accepted the court requirement that he seek counseling with a licensed counselor specializing in child abuse. He felt not quite a criminal, but almost!

Bob knew that something had gone wrong somewhere to bring him to the point where he was threatened with arrest and treated like a criminal suspect. And all he had done was to discipline his eight-year-old son who, everyone agreed, needed more discipline than most other kids. Bob escaped the public trial, redeemed his marriage, and kept his job. But by such a thin margin!

What had Bob Foreman, solid Christian father, church leader, and respected businessman done to put himself and his family at such risk? What did Bob not know about tough kids and child abuse laws?

Understanding the basics

Bob Foreman had lapses in his knowledge in two areas, and these "missing links" nearly cost him his family and his testimony.

He needed to learn something about the condition his son Barry was afflicted with and how he could better discipline him. And he needed to know something about child abuse and the law.

Barry's problem: Simply stated, eight-year-old Barry is hyperactive. He will probably grow out of it in the next few years, and because we have already discussed this disability in an earlier chapter I won't repeat the information here. But Bob, rather than Barry, was the problem in this case. Bob, as a conservative, Bible-believing Christian, had been taught all his life the importance of discipline to children. He told me during one of our sessions that "God knows *I* certainly was disciplined by *my* father when I was a boy—and *I* wasn't nearly as "bad" as Barry." A little getting even here, do you suppose? It is very common to hear adult survivors of child abuse make the kind of comment I just heard from Bob.

"I had to put up with it. Why shouldn't he have to do the same"?

"My dad beat me until I couldn't stand up and now *I'm* in trouble!"

"I didn't do nearly what my father did to me."

"How come I'm in trouble when all I did was what I was taught to do?"

These are tough questions, but I hear them often. Why *are* these fathers in trouble? They are right, really. They wouldn't have been in trouble for doing what they did 50 years, or even 20 years ago. But they are in trouble now and the law is not going to soften.

New rules for disciplining children are in effect these days and fathers like Bob and countless others are going to have to be careful to live within two laws, God's and man's. Bob Foreman knew quite a bit about the Bible and what it had to say on the subject of child discipline. Bob was familiar with passages such as Proverbs 19:18; "Discipline your son, for in that there is hope; do not be a willing party to his death."

Bob remembered the famous "spare the rod" passage from his own Sunday School lessons, the one that says "He who spares the rod hates his son, but he who loves him is careful to discipline him" (Proverbs 13:24).

The verse that most reminded Bob of his own childhood beatings was the one his father would quote to him as he was being whipped: "Do not withhold discipline from a child; if you punish him with the rod, he will not die. Punish him with the rod and save his soul from death" (Proverbs 23:13-14).

Bob had experienced a long history of beatings based on the Bible, and he was more than a little confused about why he was the first in his family to get into trouble over this practice.

The more we talked, the more I understood just where Bob was coming from. In his heart he was not happy about the beatings he had given Barry. Bob was as familiar with the words of Jesus about children as he was the Proverbs of Solomon. He had never been able to balance the passages mentioned above with the love of Jesus, especially for children.

Solomon said, "Folly is bound up in the heart of a child, but the rod of discipline will drive it far from him"(Proverbs 22:15).

Jesus, however, said, "...I will tell you the truth, you will never enter the kingdom of heaven" (Matthew 18:3).

Bob also knew that Jesus warned in several places in the Bible that "It were better for him to be thrown into the sea with a millstone tied around his neck than for him to cause one of these little ones to sin" (Luke 17:2).

Bob wondered if, in his anger at Barry's misbehavior, he might have caused his eight-year-old son to sin. Would he have to have a millstone around his neck? Would he, the father, be called to account for his treatment of his young son?

We continued our sessions exploring the issues around child abuse, and Bob grew to be able to question his own upbringing more and more. Bob had very good Christian parents who loved him very much. There wasn't any reason to doubt this. Bob knew that his father had probably been taught what he then taught Bob about disciplining children. And so it went, from generation to generation. Now it was Bob who had the dubious honor of being the first generation to be told, in no uncertain terms, that what he was doing must stop.

We talked about the fact that all Bob's lessons on child discipline came from the Old Testament. In fact, the verses came all from one book in the old testament—Proverbs.

"Isn't it odd," Bob commented one evening, "that I never realized that I was relying totally on Old Testament teachings for my child discipline principles?"

"What do you think that could mean," I asked.

"Well, I just can't help wondering if I was as balanced in disciplining Barry as I thought I was. How come those words of Jesus about loving and protecting children were left out of what I was taught? And why have I never heard our pastor talk about this? It seems that all we have heard from the pulpit is the 'spank' position and never the 'love' position. I don't get it!"

We went on to talk for several sessions about the questions that had been raised in Bob's mind. He came to realize that his pastor had probably been raised in the same discipline system as he had, so it was not surprising that the pulpit position emphasized physical correction above all else.

Eventually we arrived at the place in counseling where Bob was ready to re-think some of his beliefs and practices related to child discipline. As a part of that process, I shared the following information with him, encouraging him to work toward being more balanced in his discipline.

Research on corporal punishment

1. Boys are five to ten times more likely to be spanked or otherwise physically corrected.

We also know that the level of aggressive behavior a boy shows later on is a direct result of the severity of corporal punishment he received. In other words, a boy who learns that it is appropriate to deal with problems with physical violence (i.e., a spanking) may make the natural connection that it is then acceptable for *him* to use violence (e.g., fighting) to solve his problems.

But wait a minute! Don't assume from these comments that I am opposed to spanking. Our three children will testify to the use, though infrequent in most cases, of spanking in their early years. But this first point is valid in emphasizing the ease with which children can misinterpret what they are being taught.

Dr. James Dobson, the nationally known Christian psychologist, has stated his belief that physical methods of correction should be most commonly used in the toddler and preschool years. This kind of discipline should grow less frequent as the child grows both in body and in ability to learn the rules.

Boys and girls, but especially boys, who receive harsh or extreme physical punishment are far more likely to not only employ the same methods with their own children but also come into conflict with the law later on in life.

The equation is simple. Frequency equals violent expression of feelings later on. Intensity, or harshness of method, equals level of violence later on.

Mom or Dad, it is up to you alone to decide whether your discipline is excessive or reasonable. But whatever is decided, that parent will alone answer to God for the type and extent of punishment meted out.

2. *The more aggressive a culture, the more likely the members of that culture will be found to utilize corporal punishment as their chief socialization technique.*

Becky Waters was a single parent struggling to raise a six-year-old son on her own. Becky is a dedicated Christian who believes the Bible, and who is also firmly opposed to violence on television, war movies, cap pistols and so on.

As Becky was explaining her concerns to me in my office, she mentioned how opposed she was to young children learning about violence in a way that glorified it. I asked

Becky what she did when she discovered Derek, her six year old, had been watching a violent program without her knowing about it. Can you guess what Becky told me? She spanked him! That's right, this mom who was dead set against her son learning about "glorified" violence responded to his disobedience with violence of her own. She spanked him! I'm not sure if my jaw dropped when she told me that, but I'm afraid it did.

"Becky", I said, "Are you seriously telling me that you are trying to teach your son to avoid violent behaviors by using violent behaviors yourself? Isn't this just a little inconsistent?", I asked.

Well, Becky and I worked on this issue for a while and she seemed to make some progress in re-thinking what her response to her son might have accidentally taught. Living in a violence-oriented culture such as the United States requires Christian parents to confront the controversy head-on. There is no way around it. Violence will not be avoided, and we must be careful to think and pray about the lessons we are teaching when we parents introduce parental violence into the family equation.

3. Corporal punishment produces two primary emotions: fear and anger.

The one that has the longest "shelf-life" is anger. Long after the child has outgrown the fear of being spanked, the anger over being spanked or otherwise beaten will remain. The reality is that by the time most of us have become big enough to defend ourselves against the parent who has beaten us, we are no longer being beaten. Where then does the anger go?

What did Bob Foreman say? "I had to put up with this when I was a kid. So why should my son escape the same kind of punishment my dad used on me?" Do you hear the displaced anger in Bob's words? Can you see that the anger he felt against his father was displaced onto an acceptable target—his son Barry? This phenomenon is classic psychological displacement, and is very common in abuse cases like that of Bob Foreman, a reputable person who did not mean to break the law and was only doing what he had been taught was right.

Fear and anger. Is it any wonder that most of us have stronger positive emotions toward Mom (usually the more nurturant, non-violent parent)? Is it any wonder that those of us who were beaten by our fathers say things like, "I know my dad loved me, but he sure hit me hard when I was bad. I guess I must have deserved it." And is it any wonder that both corporal punishment and child abuse tend to run in families?

4. The level of aggression will be proportionate to that experienced by the child.

In California recently, two brothers from a wealthy Southern California family were arrested and charged with the double murder of their parents. This was a respected family, their father a prominent Hollywood attorney, their mother a socialite heavily involved in charitable work. The oldest son was a graduate of an elite "Ivy league" school and the younger son was a sophomore at a similar school on the West coast. A perfect family, some thought—until the murders were discovered.

Later, the boys were arrested and charged with the double homicides. People couldn't believe they could do such a thing. The murder had obviously been carefully planned and carried out, so much so that police initially thought the murders were mob "hits." As the case went to trial, the reality came out.

This "ideal" family was ridden with abuse. Dad would beat his wife on occasion, and would regularly whip, spank, and beat his boys. High achievers all their lives, the boys felt that they could not measure up no matter how well they did. Nothing was good enough for dad. Two weeks before the murders, dad had given the youngest son a black eye over a "C" on his grade report from college.

They'd had enough, they confessed later, and decided that the only way to escape dad's violence and have an independent life was to murder him. Mom just happened to be home unexpectedly and was killed to avoid having a witness. This is a true story, one that has not yet been resolved. Violence begets violence, and careful Christian parents will want to be judicious and sparing in their use of corporal methods. They will be equally careful to phase out physical methods as the child gets older.

How often is the story just mentioned going to happen in the average family? Rarely, of course! But the potential is always there in violent families, and we never know when that unique combination of child personality and parental beatings will result in a decision to get even when the opportunity arises.

5. *Kids who get into serious trouble are more likely to have experienced harsh and frequent physical punishment compared to those who do not get into serious trouble.*

Simply stated, delinquents tend to be physically punished more than non-delinquents. This truth is received by conservative Christians about as happily as the statistics indicating that capital punishment fails to deter murder. Nevertheless, both statements appear to be true.

Stress and Abuse

Stress, whether experienced by individual or family, encourages reactions more likely to be emotional than thoughtful, and physical rather than non-physical. Stress is experienced by all conscious human beings old enough and possessed of sufficient intellectual skills to be able to understand. Stress is universal, a permanent part of the human condition, and usually productive of negative responses by the people involved. And stress encourages child abuse.

In Bob Foreman's case, the stress was not as obvious as often found in abuse allegations. Most of the time the stress results from father's unemployment or alcoholism, the family's poverty, mom's drug use, having out-of-work relatives move in with the family and further strain family resources, or low levels of education or intelligence. Families most likely to abuse their children are much more likely to have a disabled family member, a child who is retarded or learning disabled, or live in a violent part of the city. Families where abuse is found often have parents who were married or pregnant as teenagers, are school drop-outs and unemployed or under-employed as a result. Parents in abusing families tend to be isolated from their extended family and without many friends to talk with.

But none of these stress conditions is found with Bob Foreman and his family.

In fact, Bob seems to be the direct opposite of all the characteristics. There was no drug or alcohol ever in the Foreman home, They lived in an upper-middle class neighborhood with safe streets and good schools. No one in the family was disabled, either mentally or physically. Bob was at the top of his career, far from unemployment. They did not live in crowded conditions, and they lived very close to both sets of grandparents. Bob did not fit the profile of the abusing father, with one exception. Bob is a Bible-believing, conservative Christian who believed that spanking is required of good parents trying to raise good kids. The stress that Bob experienced was "performance stress" related to his need to demonstrate to his parents and others in the church that he was a good father.

The stress Bob experienced came not from outside himself, but from within. Bob had a "performance criteria" to measure up to if he was to keep his reputation as a Christian father and church leader. Bob told me on one occasion that he knew he was out of line at times with Barry, going way overboard in his discipline, but he was worried that others in his church would see him as a weak or "liberal" father if he did not crack down on Barry, especially for church-based misbehavior.

Bob also knew that he would be perceived as disrespectful to his own father if he did not repeat the beatings he received as a child. Often overlooked when considering the psychological stress felt by conservative Christian families is the "family papacy" phenomenon, wherein one generation feels compelled to repeat the mistaken behavior of the older generation lest they be seen as being critical of that older generation. Bob said more than once, "I could not do that to my father. I could not let him know that I disagreed with the way he disciplined me as a boy and that I wasn't going to do the same thing with Barry. I just couldn't do that to him." So the abuse continued for one more generation.

Stress encourages child abuse, but the stress can be external or internal, obvious or below the surface. But stress is always involved at some level. Bob, however, experienced another kind of "performance stress," one that related more to the pastor of his church than anything else. The Foreman family had always been in conservative, fundamental/evangelical churches led by a pastor who was very much in charge of all aspects of church life and ministry. Bob's pastor, Dr. Kinmore, was a graduate of a very conservative, fundamentalist Bible college that strongly emphasized the independent church and the pastor-leader in charge. This has been a common feature of conservative, Bible-believing Christianity in this century, and was in no way unusual.

Dr. Kinmore was a true "pulpiteer," who preached with power and pulled no punches when it came to telling "his" church members what they were doing wrong and what they had better do to correct it. Bob's pastor had very strong feelings on the importance of physical punishment for misbehavior in children *and adolescents* and would often proclaim that no family in "his" church was going to grow kids to become "long-haired hippies, drug-crazed weirdos, or general reprobates." Not if they did what he told those families to do, anyway!

And for the most part, Dr. Kinmore was correct. The families in his church did not produce such children, and he firmly believed it was more the result of the spankings he recommended than anything else. Unfortunately, Dr. Kinmore was about as equally ignorant of what the Bible really says (or more importantly, does *not* say) about child discipline as he was of current child abuse legislation. If Bob Foreman had a pastor who was correctly informed about these matters, he would not have had to go through what he did with the child abuse allegations.

This is not to excuse Bob of his responsibility, of course. I am just trying to point out the importance of the content of the pulpit messages we hear. It is critical for families not only to be involved, as the New Testament church of Berea was, in "searching the Scriptures daily." But they also need to know for themselves what legal restrictions may relate to their discipline practices. The fact of the matter is that we cannot discipline our children as we please. The laws on child abuse are nation-wide, and without exception.

Stumbling-blocks or Stepping-stones

Bob Foreman is not very different from you and me. What helped Bob re-think his situation was a question I asked regarding how he saw himself and his discipline practices. I asked Bob to consider whether or not those practices would help Barry be a better person, or perhaps be worse off.

In other words, were the whippings applied to this eight year old going to prove to be stepping-stones that would direct his path toward God and a good Christian life, or stumbling-blocks that would hinder his growth in the Lord?

Bob thought about this for several weeks as we discussed it off and on during the counseling sessions. He couldn't be sure, he told me finally.

"No, I just can't feel sure that I was doing the right thing for my son. I thought I was, but now I see that much of what got Barry into trouble was not his fault. I wasn't helping him grow spiritually by trying to beat the devil out of him."

Tough kids like Barry desperately need to learn good self-discipline. The question in his dad's mind is the same one I hope is in yours. What is good discipline?

The next chapter will try and answer this question for you.

Love-based Discipline for Tough Kids

Good kids require good discipline. Tough kids require even better discipline!

We have seen in chapters three and four that discipline will not always be effective. There are some kids for whom normal discipline will work. Remember Carter Robbins, the fourteen year old run-away who required a time living away from his family in order to be convinced that it was in his own best interest to conform to his parents' expectations?

Shauna Houston and Allen Combes were just kids, but they were such problems that their parents nearly gave up on them. Remember Danny Whitcomb, who was difficult almost from the day he was born, and never got any easier? Danny, who tried to set his own home on fire and who was eventually diagnosed as an "unattached" child. And little Darrell Kravchuk, who killed neighborhood pets and who lived for a year in an institution for emotionally disturbed children. Even though he has improved, Darrell will probably always be a concern for his parents.

For some children, ordinary discipline will not be effective.

But for most, the rules of good discipline will prove to work, and work well. We'll begin this examination of discipline for tough kids with some optimistic thoughts.

Bad behavior is correctable in most "normal" children.

No child is born knowing how to misbehave. It must be learned.

Yes, the motivation to misbehave is inherent in all human beings, but the method of their misbehavior must be acquired somewhere along the way. Because of this apparent truth, it naturally follows that what is learned can be unlearned. No simplistic statement is going to negate the hard work involved in helping kids "un-learn" attitudes and behavior. But it can be done. Will we experience failures in our efforts to re-teach better behavior to children? Of course. The families discussed in earlier chapters attest to that.

But optimism is essential. The American Psychological Association will not allow therapists and diagnosticians to apply certain labels to children under eighteen—labels that would be appropriate in adults. Why? Because youngsters are assumed to have the potential for change, whereas adults lose that potential with age. Unacceptable behavior can be corrected.

Any authoritative adult can do the correcting

What is an authoritative adult? It's a good question, but hard to answer. A witness testifying before a Senate committee on pornography was asked for his definition of "pornography." He answered "I don't know if I can define it for you, but I know it when I see it."

I think the same applies to defining what is authoritative

and what is not. Let me refer back to my public school teaching in Detroit. There was great variety in our faculty. We were about equally divided between black and white, male and female, and in this group of about 42 teachers we had some great disciplinarians and some who were very poor in that area. But what surprised me was that it was impossible to me, as a new teacher in those days, to predict which teacher would maintain good discipline and which would not.

Mr. Ogden taught English in room 308. He was a former professional football player with the Cleveland Browns who had returned to his home city of Detroit to teach. Mr. Ogden was immense. Huge. Well over six feet tall, and easily weighing 260 pounds. He was the stereotypical former football player. Somewhat gone to fat, but nonetheless intimidating by his presence alone.

Miss Szymanski taught Math down in Room 122. A woman who looked for all the world as though she should have been a nun, Rose Szymanski did not stand five-feet four or weigh more than 120 pounds. She had never married, and saw teaching as her calling in life.

Both teachers were equally dedicated to teaching. But Miss Szymanski *never* sent a kid to the office for disciplinary reasons. She was never known to raise her voice, much less strike a child—even in those days, when corporal punishment was still allowed.

Mr. Ogden, however—*huge* Mr. Ogden—had a terrible time with discipline. He consistently sent two or three kids down to the assistant principal's office from each class throughout the day. Mr. Ogden *did* get physical with the kids once in a while—not so much paddling as picking kids up physically to remove them from the room, for example.

During my years at Wilson Junior High School, Mr. Ogden gained a reputation for being a pushover in class.

But Miss Szymanski was known as "The Iron Maiden" for her calm, resolute toughness. Can these differences be explained? Maybe. There was something very different about these two teachers that was related to their ability to discipline effectively. I believe Rose Szymanski had acquired self-confidence as a teacher, and that self-confidence impacted her ability to discipline and maintain classroom control without ever touching a child in anger—and usually by just staring at a misbehaving adolescent. Boy could she stare! She would cross her arms and get right in the miscreants' face and stare at them until they wilted. The kids started a rumor that Miss Szymanski never blinked.

Miss Szymanski was also voted the teacher of the year for two of the seven years I was at Wilson. Mr. Ogden never even came close. So what is it to be an authoritative adult? I don't know for sure, but I know it when I see it, and so do you, I'll bet!

Most behavior is easily correctable without resorting to physical methods

You already know that I am not opposed to spanking in the family. But at the same time, I am worried about the overuse of physical methods that could easily lead to emotional side-effects.

Rose Szymanski never touched a kid, yet she was a wonderful disciplinarian. Mr. Ogden got physical often but had terrible discipline problems. Good parents can discipline with or without the use of physical methods. Bad parents are unable to discipline effectively no matter what method they use. The method is not the issue so much as the parent on the other end.

Linda and I have a wheelchair-bound friend who is a wife

and mother. She does not have the physical strength to use spanking and other physical methods, yet her children are very well-behaved. This lady has been able to communicate power to her children through her character and parental role alone. Even when her husband is unavailable to help, her children respond to her voice and her eyes. They *know* they must do as she asks.

Yet we see parents in super markets and elsewhere who slap and shake their children with absolutely no effect—except to make the children misbehave even more. Corporal methods can be effective but there is more to the discipline equation.

How to prevent MOST serious discipline problems

1. Understand that parenting (including good discipline) is not inherited as hair color and other physical traits, but is learned in the process of growing up.

Therefore, parents who pay close attention to day-to-day activities with their children are much less likely to experience a seriously misbehaving child or teenager.

A guarantee? Of course not! But if we accept the truth of Proverbs 22:6 related to the importance of early training, we will understand that good parenting always involves good discipline, and that the combination of these two will prevent most serious behavior problems later on. (Most—not all!)

2. Understand the value of self-discipline as we serve as role models for our children.

Parents who are able to delay their own gratification will have a much easier time teaching their children to wait for things.

Consider the mother of a fourteen-year-old who has the task of trying to convince her daughter to refrain from sex when the mother herself became pregnant before she was married. Can this be done well? Yes! But the mom in this case will have to use her experiences to help her daughter understand the costs involved in such decisions. And there is always the risk that, no matter what mom says or how well she has lived her life since those days, her experience as a young woman may be interpreted by her daughter as tacit permission to risk the same outcomes.

Parents who can wait for rewards will be more likely to have children who can wait for rewards. That's not very complicated, but it's very important. Parents who are self-controlled and Spirit-led demonstrate for their children those same values that should enable them to get what God wants for them in life. Free-will is at work here as well, so we cannot be absolutist about end results.

3. *Provide structure.*

That's such a simple statement but so difficult for so many families to do. Structure in the home is not very different from structure in the workplace. It simply means that family members know where they are to be, at what time, and what they are to be doing, and what will happen if they do, or don't do, what is expected.

Structure, as we are discussing it here, is a health-giving aspect of good families. It is not meant to become oppressive and legalistic. I know of too many families run like military boot camps (the father is often a former military man). This always results in problems—if not in childhood, in adolescence, for sure.

Structure in a family communicates security to the children by letting them know that mom and dad are really in charge. Structure means that kids know what is expected of them, regardless of whether or not they believe the expectations are fair. Structure is another of the "warm fuzzies" children need so much if they are to grow up unafraid and self-confident.

But excessive structure is to be avoided at all costs. This legalistic, oppressive form of family control tells the children that one or the other of their parents is frightened, so the children become frightened too. Excessive rules and regulations always stem from fear of something. Parents who are this way are frightened of being seen as weak or incompetent, or they are scared that their children will eventually rise up and take over. Parents in this category tend to produce children who are like mice and teenagers who are like monsters.

4. *Become involved in the child's life.*

This may seem a little silly to some. Many of us wonder if we are too involved in our children. Certainly, over-involvement is to be avoided. It can lead to what psychology calls "enmeshment," where one or both parents are living out their lives through the lives of their child. This is the dad who is getting his life's sense of significance through his son's high school football exploits. Or it can be seen in the "stage mother" who signs up her daughter for every talent show and beauty pageant available.

But within normal parameters, parents are to be involved with their children.

Parents should attend the special events in their child or teenager's life—athletic events, recitals, spelling bees, and so on. We want to communicate involvement, but not exploitation. Exploitation means that a parent expects the child or teen to meet the parent's needs rather than supporting the child or teen as their needs are met through the activity.

When in doubt ask!

If you are wondering if you go to too many games or special events, just ask your child or teen if they would rather you skip one now and then. This kind of question will also help a parent understand if the channels of communication are really open.

5. Develop and practice two-way communication.

Answer the following questions with a "yes" or "no."

_____1.   My child or teen appears to be listening to what I say.

_____2.   When I am not understood, or if I do not understand, I get clarification before I go any further.

_____3.   When I talk with my child or teen, I keep in mind their developmental level.

_____4.   I try to ask questions and talk "inductively" so as to bring my child or teen into the subject being discussed.

_____5.   I earn the right to be listened to by listening.

_____6.   I try to speak rationally rather than emotionally.

_____7.   In every-day interaction with my child or teen, I listen about as much as I talk.

_____8.   When communication fails, I understand what happened.

_____9.   I am able to help my child or teen express their feelings verbally.

_____10.   I can say no.

_____11.   Conflicts and arguments are resolved.

_____12.   I am conscious of what my child or teen wants to hear.

_____13.   I am a self-controlled, Spirit-led communicator.

If you honestly answered most of these questions with a "yes," congratulations! You are very unlikely to find yourself in a major battle with a child or teenager. (No guarantees, remember.) But we know what works, and open-ended, two-way communication based on love and respect just cannot lose.

6. *Focus on positive behavior.*

We parents are so greatly impacted by the kind of parenting we experienced as we were growing up that we sometimes fail to notice what we are doing.

Being raised by a negative parent will surely increase the chances that the next generation will be equally negative in *their* parenting. Seeing the glass half-empty rather than half-full is a terrible burden to place on the shoulders of any youngster. But putting the emphasis on positive behavior, having an optimistic and hopeful outlook on life, is equally beneficial to children and teens.

Parents who can focus on positive behaviors tend to produce children with higher self concepts, and a higher self concept leads to an achievement-orientation, a willingness to take a risk and tackle a big challenge, and most of all, the belief that God is an optimist.

7. *Keep your sense of humor.*

Notice that I didn't say "get" a sense of humor. A sense of humor is one of those qualities that you either are born with or will never experience. In fact, if you do not have a sense of humor, these words you are reading right now are not making sense to you! In any case, a sense of humor will pull you through many dark and gloomy parenting experiences. Having the ability to laugh at your situation is both a tension-reliever and a mental health builder. Neurologists have proven that a chemical is released in the brain in response to intense "belly-laughs" that replicates the feeling produced by some tranquilizers.

I personally know of a cancer specialist who prescribes certain old-time comedy films for his patients. He may prescribe one day of chemo-therapy followed by other medicines to be taken in conjunction with two "Laurel and Hardy" films.

But never laugh at your teens or their troubles. And it is probably not a good idea to try to get them to laugh with you. That's okay! They're teenagers, after all! But we parents *need* to be able to laugh in order to maintain our sanity.

8. Work at strengthening your marriage.

A good marriage is obviously important when viewed from God's perspective. After all, it was he who proclaimed "till death them do part." Having a good marriage is important because God said it was. But beyond that, and in more every-day terms, a good marriage provides security for growing children. And it teaches them what to do when they marry.

It should come as no surprise that one solid predictor of divorce-risk is the marital history of one's parents. Having a good marriage also helps mom and dad present a united front when it comes time to hand down a "no" decision to a teenager. The principle learned by every teen with two parents is "divide and conquer," and parents who are not getting along with each other are prime targets for exploitation by children and teens.

9. Stay up-to-date on current events and problems.

Mom or dad, do you know what is current in the teenage music scene? If your teenager makes a comment about the new cassette just purchased, will you know whether or not to be concerned? Are you current on the new terms for drugs, sex, and alcohol?

It's true confessions time. Because of the counseling work I do and the amount of time I spend with Christian families struggling with a teenager, I watch some music television. That's right! The stuff your kids turn off as soon as you walk into the living room. I need to do this because I *must* be current. I do *not* enjoy the great majority of what I see and hear, but I feel unprepared for working with teenagers in this day and age—even Christian teens—without this experience.

I equate this with what a police officer might have to read or listen to in order to do his job properly. It's unpleasant, yes. But a careful Christian parent will want to be aware of the world a teenager faces.

10. Understand that these kids are not yours.

I know we have already discussed this, but its importance bears repetition. Your children and mine are God's creation, not ours. They did not begin nor will they end with us. We are not their owners. We are their stewards. Place the responsibility where it belongs—with God, their Creator.

We parents are the tools God has chosen to use, but we are only children ourselves. We cannot understand the Bible perfectly because we think with sin-riddled brains. We cannot be perfect parents, and God does not expect that from us. God expects us to be careful stewards of the children He has placed into our hands.

Our trust is in Him and not ourselves. He alone knows the end from the beginning, and we parents are just one part of God's plan for the life of our child. Trust Him.

Rules for effective discipline

The following comments apply to more "every-day" discipline problems. Many of the children you have read about in this book needed something "extraordinary" when it came to discipline. In several cases it was beyond their parent's ability to supply what they needed.

These "rules" of effective discipline *will* work with the vast majority of youngsters, and they should be tried first before going to alternate methods. These work! We know that, but it could be that your child needs a little more. You will quickly see if they fit your child or teen.

Benjamin Lipscomb was only seven years old, and was already a concern to his parents. Benny, as he was usually called, didn't seem the threat to his parents' sanity they described. I assumed the Benny I just met in the office that Tuesday was on his very best behavior.

Benny and I talked about school and friends for a few minutes and then I asked "Benny, why do you think your mom and dad brought you here to see me today?"

"I get bad sometimes," he replied, head down and looking at the floor as if he was already in trouble.

"Bad? What kind of bad do you mean, Benny?"

"Oh, I don't know for sure. I tell everybody that I don't mean to be bad, but I just keep getting into trouble all the time. I guess there's something wrong with me or something. I don't know for sure."

This was a troubled kid talking to me. Clearly, Benny did not get into trouble at school—we had already checked with his teachers. But Benny was really punishing himself for the trouble he got into at home. I assured this little boy that I would try real hard to help him and his parents figure out what was going on at home. I promised we would try to help him stay out of trouble at home, as he did in school.

Benny's parents made an appointment for the following week and I asked them to come in without their son. What I learned about the Lipscomb family has stayed with me for several years and allowed me to help dozens of other families with the same type of problem.

Benny and his discipline

Most of what Benny did that got him into trouble

happened when his dad was away at work. Instead of his mom dealing with him when he misbehaved, she would tell Benny, "Wait 'till your father gets home."

Benny had no choice but to wait. Where was a seven-year-old kid going to go? The trouble was that Benny had mostly forgotten the bad stuff he did by the time dad pulled in the driveway. Benny would get scolded or spanked, depending on how dad's day at work had gone. Once spanked, mom and dad would give him a hug. (He never could figure out why he was getting hugs when he had just been spanked or hollered at.) Then the family would go for an ice cream cone.

Benny and his sisters wondered why it was that a spanking to any one of them almost guaranteed an ice cream cone for all of them.

"Discipline sure can be confusing," thought Benny. He was also confused because it didn't seem to matter what he did to earn discipline. His dad seemed to spank, scold, take away television time or the skateboard in no relation to how bad Benny's behavior had been. Stuff that Benny thought he would get killed for doing was sometimes overlooked. At other times, minor offenses got him a serious spanking.

What did Benny learn about discipline? Not much that was good, I'm afraid! Let's examine some of the mistakes Benny's parents made in their discipline.

1. *Benny was made to wait for the discipline.*

Some would say that making a kid wait to get spanked, grounded, or any of the other discipline options available to parents, is "cruel and unusual punishment."

Benny's mom should have gone ahead and corrected his behavior right away, following the principle that the quicker the discipline, the better the learning. But she didn't. She said "Wait 'till your father gets home." This diluted her power and influence, and virtually assured that dad would be in a foul mood all evening. No parent, mom or dad, wants to be greeted with a problem as soon as he or she steps in the door. And it was clear that the anger in Benny's father was as much directed at Benny's mom as it was at Benny. The boy should have been disciplined right away by whichever parent was available.

2. *The discipline Benny received did not always match what he did wrong.*

Sometimes Benny did really bad things and nothing much happened. At other times, what he did was almost an accident, but he really caught it!

The inconsistency Benny experienced was as much the responsibility of his mother as it was his father's fault. Mom should have cleared up family emergencies before dad arrived home. When she didn't, the discipline delivered was more controlled by dad's day at work and how he felt at the moment, and this is wrong.

Discipline must be both reasonable (making the punishment fit the crime) and consistent. Benny's discipline was neither. As a result, Benny did not learn as much as he should have, and the behavior that got him into trouble in the first place is more likely to happen again as a result.

3. *Benny's parents mixed rewards with punishment.*

After the spanking came the hugs and trips to the ice cream store. Were Benny's parents trying to create a sado-masochist out of their son? Of course not. But they acted as if they were! When parents follow discipline with rewards like hugs and ice cream cones, kids learn that mom and dad feel guilty about the discipline they just delivered. Why else, reasons the seven-year-old brain, would they try to make me feel better after first making me feel bad?

Unfortunately, many people are presently burdened with confusion about the relationship between violence and love.

Some wives think their husbands do not love them unless they get "smacked around" once in a while. Some husbands believe their wives expect beatings as a sign that they are loved. And some children grow up thinking that love and violence go together in families.

Of course Benny's parents were not thinking of all these potential problems resulting from careless discipline. But that's just the point. They should have been thinking rather than striking out.

4. *Benny's discipline was "grace-less."*

It would have been really nice if once in a while Benny's dad would have said "Oh, forget about it son. I know you didn't mean it. " Benny never heard those words. Not once! There was no grace or forgiveness in the discipline he received; just revenge and showing the kids who was the boss. Benny was not even allowed to apologize for what he had done, because his dad was too quick. Before Benny could go out and apologize, they were in the car and on their way to the ice cream store.

5. *And worst of all, at least to Benny, was the feeling he got from his mom and dad that they really expected him to "mess up."*

There was no apparent optimism in Benny's family, at least not when it came to the kids. I didn't learn very much about Benny's sisters, but I would be greatly surprised if they too did not become "discipline problems" just as their brother had. Benny told me he just didn't feel that he could ever be good enough for his parents. An expectation of failure had been created in this little boy, and he was being pressed down by it. Already his self-concept was beginning to wilt, and there was no reason to expect that the situation would improve. Unless his parents did some fast, new learning about child discipline, the outlook for Benny is not very good!

How to be a family "Commander"

Benny's mom and dad were not very good at being disciplinarians. But it wouldn't have taken very much effort on their part to become good family "commanders." The following suggestions for improving family discipline apply mainly to families with younger children, but the lesson is that what is practiced early bears good fruit immediately, and for many years after, even through adolescence. Here's how!

1. Give commands clearly and only once!

When the command is given, the parent stands there in front of the child maintaining eye contact and *waiting* for the child to comply with the parent's command. Too many parents tell a child to do something, then walk away or turn and do something else.

What do we expect children to think when mom or dad gives a command and then walks away as if it didn't matter? A physical presence looming over their small body is very powerful. It conveys *POWER!* It says "I mean for you to do it *NOW!*"

If there is any doubt about the command just given, ask the child to repeat it back to you to make sure he or she understood.

And then stay there at least until they begin. Don't walk away.

Let me identify some examples of vague, unclear commands that tend to give kids problems, and some other examples of good, clear, exact commands that are much easier for kids to understand and respond to.

Good Commands	Vague, Unclear Commands
1. Ask me before you take a cookie.	1. Be considerate of others.

2. Listen carefully to what I am going to tell you.	2. Pay attention.
3. Now repeat back to me what I just told you to do.	3. Do as you are told.
4. Do not interrupt us while we are talking.	4. Behave yourself.
5. Do your homework *NOW*, and show me what you have done at six o'clock.	5. Work hard.

2. Avoid chain commands.

Remember that you are talking to a child with an immature, still developing brain. He or she has limited ability to remember and understand. Don't tell your nine year old to "clean up your closet, take out the trash in your wastebasket, wash your hands and face, brush your teeth, and then you can go out to play with your friends."

Could *you* remember all that when you were nine?

You probably don't even remember *being* nine! Tell your child, "clean up your room and then report to me for further instructions," etc. This is not rocket science I know, but as simple as it appears, it works!

3. Avoid question commands.

Kids need clarity and power in their parents, as well as love. Parents should not say to a child, "Wouldn't you like to take your bath now?" The sharp five year old will reply, "No!" This is not disobedience or rebellion. This is just a child answering a question from a parent. So he doesn't want to

162

take his bath. You asked, didn't you? What did you expect? "Yes, mommy, I would just love to hop in that hot bathtub stark naked and be scrubbed within an inch of my life."

4. *Avoid "Let's" commands.*

"Let's get ready for school, shall we?" can bring the reply, "No, you go ahead, mom. I'll catch up with you in a few minutes."

It's a small point perhaps, but if used repeatedly, these types of commands convey to the sharp child that the parent really does not know what they are doing. Most of us have spent some time in a hospital and been exposed to the nurse or aid who asks, "Are we ready for our surgery tomorrow?" or "How are we feeling today?" Isn't it strange that we do to our children some of the very things that annoy us so much?

5. *Avoid commands followed by a rationale.*

"Get dressed Billy, we have to go to Grandma's house," or "C'mon, Billy! Get up. You'll be late for school," or "Clean up your room, Billy, company's coming over tonight."

Do these all sound innocent? Do they sound like something you have heard others do all your life? Does it sound like a disaster just waiting to happen? *Giving explanations for commands teaches innocent children to expect a reason for a command.* All goes well until the first time mom or dad says "Billy, clean up your toys." and Billy says "Why should I?"

BOOM!

Well, c'mon mom and dad, haven't you trained Billy to expect a reason? Why are you getting upset when he does exactly what you have trained him to do? Of course we don't *mean* to do this, but all too often we do it anyway. Early experiences with discipline, good or bad, set a pattern that will probably last a lifetime. Whatever mistakes we practice with our children will probably be passed on to our grandchildren. And on and on.

But there is an up-side to this, too. In most families, the good that parents do far outweighs the bad. What is needed more than lessons for parents is awareness by parents of those aspects of disciplining children and teens known to be important.

Lessons are fine. Books and seminars are helpful. But parent awareness is critical.

The self-disciplined parent

We have touched on this idea previously, but I think the concept of the "self-disciplined disciplinarian" is a good review for this chapter.

We are reminded of the overwhelming power of the parent-model in the life of a child. The most outstanding teacher will never be as influential as the most "average" parent. We parents teach by what we do and by what we do not do. Parents teach by mere presence and by manifest absence. We teach how to live, love, laugh, and be happy. We show our children how to understand and deal with God. Or how to run from God. We teach them how to be with others in hundreds of different situations. Our teaching defies limitation and explanation. It can only be good or bad.

So it is with discipline.

We teach by example, and not by word. What we *say* matters hardly at all. What we *do* makes all the difference in the world. We parents are teachers till the day we die, and sometimes for many years after that.

Brutal discipline teaches brutality, and is passed from father to son to grandson. Loving, compassionate discipline is also passed from generation to generation, and results in love and understanding that grows with each new generation of child learners.

As I have matured in understanding and I have grown more sensitive to God's expectations of me as a father, I have tried to become a self-disciplined parent. If you have not been self-disciplined in raising your children, fix it now before it is too late.

God bless you as you become the most self-disciplined disciplinarian you can be.

Doing the best we can

In the long run, the example we set as parents matters most.

We sometimes fool ourselves into thinking that our words have more power than our actions, that children pay more attention to the lectures we give than the life we live. But this is never the case. What we say matters, but only in the context of living proof behind those words. I have met with and counseled scores of Christian parents and, with each new visit, I expect to hear "We are doing the best we can. What else can we do?"

Many of us *are* doing the best we can. We are doing all we know to do, but answers seem to slip away from us anyway. The issue is not that we should do better, or that we could do better. This is always true. As long as imperfection is the norm, perfection will be an unreached goal.

You and I live in a sinful world, and we struggle with our sinful selves and sinful kids. We try to understand what is happening, then formulate a plan of action despite the limited and sin-afflicted brain we were born with. The sad truth is that we will not always find an answer to what our kids are going through. A few of our kids will experience a lifetime of struggles of their own making—and even they won't know why they continue to self-destruct.

Some of us will spend countless dollars searching for an answer that never reveals itself because there is no answer beyond what God has said. All have sinned. All are sinning. All will sin in the future. What do we expect, mom and dad? Do we expect that our kids will not fail in the trial and error process of growing up? Do we think that we, with our limited understanding, will be able to figure out why our teenager or grown child continues to live a life of sin?

Prodigals abound! They always have; they always will. But it seems to have fallen to this generation of Christian parents to take on the responsibility for the behavior of their prodigal. I apologize for the strong tone of these words. I say them as much to myself as to you. Look at the story of the prodigal son in Luke 15:11-32.

The son intentionally ignored the advice of his father and decided to take his inheritance early and leave for the land of perpetual partying. His father not only allowed him to leave, he financed the trip by granting him his inheritance. Did the father have a choice? Absolutely! These are Bible times don't forget, when a father's word was law. What did this father know that you and I may not know? Could it be that his son was well taught in spiritual principles, and that the father knew that he could not leave those early lessons behind?

Many Bible scholars think this is the real message of Proverbs 22:6: "Train a child in the way he should go, and when he is old he will not turn from it." It has been noted that the word we translate "turn from" could better mean "voluntarily ignore" or "leave behind."

The truth is that this prodigal child was just like yours or mine, if we have raised him or her in the nurture and admonition of the Lord. They *cannot* forget what they learned in the early years. Perhaps this father also knew that God was truly in charge of this young man's destiny. He also may have realized that his son, knowing that he *could* come back, probably *would* come back some day.

How do we know if we are doing the best we can with our tough kids? The prophet Haggai warned the people of God: "This is what the LORD Almighty says: 'Give careful thought to your ways' " (Haggai 1:5).

Ways! The most common meaning of "ways" used in the Bible is "the well-trodden path of one's life." The idea is related to the daily life we live before our children and God. That walk cannot lie as words can. This is one's lifestyle, the pattern that is most typical of a person. It means the direction one's life is taking, the ultimate goal, the thing we would most like to have accomplished before we die.

"Ways" can be summed up in what our children would write on our tombstone right now if given the opportunity. I have listened to the most dysfunctional kids imaginable tell me that though they totally disagreed with the religious orientation of their parents, yet they admired and respected them for living what they believed. Parents such as this simply had "ways" that were consistent with their religious beliefs.

This concept seems so easy to say, but it's so hard when one counts the number of parents who fail to consider their ways. Our ways as parents can be so important that God tells us He will not listen to us nor answer our prayers until we turn from our wicked ways (see II Chronicles 7:14). A little further on in that same book, we find King Josiah being complimented for following the "ways" of King David, his ancestor. "And he [King Josiah] did what was right in the eyes of the LORD and walked in the ways of David, his father, not turning aside to the right or to the left" (II Chronicles 34:2).

But wait a minute. Wasn't David a murderer and an adulterer? Didn't he experience the death of a son because of his immoral relationship with Bathsheba? These couldn't be the "ways" that Josiah followed! Of course not.

But this points out that *our ways can change*, as David's did—so significantly that this adulterer and murderer would be known throughout history as a man after God's own heart. David changed his wicked ways, and God did restore him, though the scars of David's sin remained with him throughout his life.

But if we are going to be careful Christian parents, we are going to have to get more specific. For this we turn to Jeremiah 17:10: "I, the LORD search the heart and examine the mind, to reward a man according to his conduct, according to what his deeds deserve."

If we examine this passage carefully, we find three major areas of concern that gets God's attention. First, God searches the heart to see what we desire. What would we ask for if we had a magic wand that really worked? Our children learn of this part of our ways by doing nothing more than living in the family. What does dad want out of life? Does he tithe willingly or does he complain about being expected to "pay God"? Are mom and dad really committed to each other and the sanctity of their marriage?

Millions of fathers in America have said to their children "I really love you. I just don't love your mother anymore, and so I'm leaving." You can't fool kids. They know that if dad or mom *really* loved them as much as they claim they would put the needs of children above their own "desires" and stay together for the children's sake.

What do you *desire*, mom and dad? What is in your heart of

hearts that you would wish for if you had only one wish and knew that you would get what was requested?

Not sure? Okay, what do you spend time on? What do you talk about most? Envy most? Worry about most? These are "the desires of the heart" that God pays so much attention to.

Secondly, God also "examines the mind" to see what we think about. God is no puppet master; we can think about whatever we wish. But we can't fool our kids. They will always figure out if we really mean what we are saying, or if our words are for "public relations."

Mom and dad, what do you read most? Do we spend more time reading news magazines or television schedules than the Bible? I'm not meddling here. Your thoughts are none of my business, and I know it. But the thought content of parents is extremely important in teaching their children what they, too, should spend time thinking about.

Many Christian dads talk about sports as though these games were really important to them. What's their child to think about that? Many Christian moms are current on every death, divorce, and deceit of afternoon "soap operas," but feel incompetent to teach a Sunday School class of four-year-old kids!

What's their child supposed to think? I'll tell you what! A child will think whatever mom and dad think. This is precisely why God is so emphatic in telling us to "consider our ways." If dad spends 99 percent of his waking hours thinking, talking, watching, and participating in sports, you can be equally 99 percent sure that junior will grow up to do likewise. Of course the same applies for mothers and daughters.

God, speaking through the prophet Jeremiah, tells us to be careful what we think about. *God examines our heart*. The message is simple. The application is crucial.

And the third element in Jeremiah's reminder relates to "what our deeds deserve." *Results*, in modern terms.

What is the product of your life to this point? Of course you are not finished yet, and it would be unfair for God to evaluate you or me now. Or would it? True, the basic message of Jeremiah 17:10 has to do with the end of one's life, but the one-quarter, half-way, etc. mileposts must be important, too.

They are. Our kids may say some day, "Well, I know dad grouched about the preacher's sermons a lot. But after all, dad was always in church, wasn't he?" Another might say, "Yes, mom was stingy and tight with money, no question about it. But I know that she saved so that she could support mission projects, and in that sense she was generous." The day before you die, mom or dad, how will your kids evaluate your life? I wonder if we care as much as God does!

The encouragement of Job

It is easy to begin feeling like a worm of the earth rather than a child of the King when it comes to parenting. A passage in Job comes to mind. In Job 1:4-5, we find this hero of the faith worrying about his own grown kids.

This is the man God was willing to trust in a battle against Satan himself! But we read: "His sons used to take turns holding feasts in their homes, and they would invite their three sisters to eat and drink with them. When a period of feasting had run its course, Job would send and have them purified. Early in the morning he would sacrifice a burnt offering for each of them, thinking, 'Perhaps my children have sinned and cursed God in their hearts.' This was Job's regular custom."

Job was worried that his grown children may have sinned and was making sacrifice in their behalf. This same Job who wrote one of the boldest statements found in the Bible: "Though he slay me, yet will I hope in him; *I will surely defend my ways to his face*" (Job 13:15).

Job, a truly humble man, is not boasting. Each of us has the power to make decisions we know to be in the general direction God wants us to move, and we should not be shy in acknowledging that we followed the directions given to us. This is what Job was doing in "defending" his ways before God. Doing "the best we can" implies an awareness of the powerful and permanent impact parents have on children. Let me suggest four primary "windows" through which our children learn of our ways.

Salvation

In Paul's second letter to young Timothy (II Timothy 1:7-8), we find encouragement to share our salvation experience. Paul writes "For God did not give us a spirit of timidity, but a spirit of power, of love and of self-discipline. So do not be ashamed to testify about our Lord, or ashamed of me his prisoner. But join with me in suffering for the gospel, by the power of God...." Along with Timothy, we are reminded that we are to be unafraid, full of power and love, and happy to share what the Lord has done for us.

Mom and dad, have your children heard the story of how you came to know Jesus as personal Savior? I often find that people in the church know more about our spiritual history than our own children do. This should not be. Find a way to share your testimony with your children and expect future benefits to follow.

Service

We are not saved by works. But works provide the proof of one's spiritual condition. What do our children know about our record of service for God and people? Think about that obituary again, the one that your children would write on the day you die. What would they say about your service for God? Anything? What would they know about your tithing and giving record? Have they ever seen you volunteer time and energy to help someone you could not gain from? Have your children seen you go to church, or have they waved goodbye to you as you dropped them off?

We have heard about Daniel in the lions' den since we were children, but there's a lesson there for adults too. In Daniel 6:16, we read the words of King Darius who is about to turn Daniel into cat chow. Darius apparently didn't want to do this but was pressured by the legal experts of his day. His parting words are recorded for us: "So the king gave the order, and they brought Daniel and threw him into the lions' den. The king said to Daniel, 'May your God, *whom you serve continually,* [emphasis mine] rescue you!' "

Would our children say about us what King Darius said about Daniel—that the God you serve continually will deliver you? We know God delivered Daniel, and I wonder if my children or yours know how God has delivered each of us, and from what. We miss a rare opportunity when we fail to live a life of service before our children.

Conversely, a life of happy, chosen service teaches volumes to children that no mere words can do. Attending church as a duty rather than a privilege teaches Christian responsibility but omits joy. Tithing grudgingly teaches that mom and dad gave, but because they had to and not because they wanted to. Praying at meals hurriedly and in a perfunctory tone teaches recognizing God's provision for us but fails to teach anything about fellowshipping with God.

Linda and I were saved as adults, and we can say that our children went with us to church on an every-week basis at least. They know that we felt privileged to be there. True, works is not the primary measure by which our children measure our spirituality. But they cannot forget what they have seen in us over the years.

Stand

Children learn about our ways from the stands we take. Perhaps you have had limited opportunities to take a stand. Maybe you live in a conservative area of the country where the battles over homosexual rights, abortion, or school prayer have not yet arrived. If so, count your blessings! But also get ready, because it won't last.

Paul warned the Ephesian church about standing up against the enemy. In Ephesians 6:13 he wrote: "Therefore put on the full armor of God, so that when the day of evil comes, you may be able to stand your ground, and after you have done everything, to stand."

We are talking about critical incidents here, moments of truth when a choice was required. Paul is thinking of a moment of truth when action would reveal thoughts and intents of the heart.

Perhaps you were given too much change back at the fast food counter and you let your child know it. Did you return it?

A moment of truth! Maybe you were driving with your family in the car and were pulled over for speeding. Did you admit your error and thank the officer for the ticket, or did you try to lie your way out of it? A moment of truth!

Perhaps your teenage son was with you when you were trying to sell a car to a stranger. When the stranger asked if the car had ever been wrecked, did you conceal the fender bender two years ago? Or did you tell the truth and risk losing the sale?

A moment of truth! Unfortunately, many children know more about the "chinks" in a parent's armor than they do about the armor itself.

Submission

James, the brother of Jesus, knew the nature of human beings when he wrote, "Submit yourselves, then, to God. Resist the devil, and he will flee from you"(James 4:7).

The obvious question as we consider the impact of parental lifestyle on children is, are we parents submitting ourselves to God—and are we resisting evil? Challenges and temptations are not the question here. *The concern is with the battle, and not the war.* We know who will win. We have read the final chapter and we know the devil eventually loses. But the question relates to individual battles and skirmishes we all face.

What do our children know about our ability to resist evil? If we are going to be successful in resisting the devil, we will do so based solely on our willingness to submit ourselves to God.

Flip Wilson, a popular comedian in the seventies, became famous proclaiming, "The devil made me do it!" What nonsense! God tells us that we can do all things through Him. We don't need to make excuses that won't fool our kids anyway.

Realizing Your Parent Power

As we draw this discussion of tough kids to a conclusion, I want to offer some mind-set suggestions that have helped me deal with my tough kids. They may help you with yours.

Even if your kids are not of the tough or super-tough variety, you can surely help other parents who are faced with challenging kids. But please remember, sometimes nothing works! Sometimes prodigal sons or daughters must experience the natural consequences of their actions before God can complete His work in their heart.

This is sad and painful for parents. I know—I have been there! But Linda and I also know that God wants us to preserve our sanity, our marriage, our testimony, and our ability to parent the other kids. I believe these suggestions will help. They are based on some of the points made briefly in chapter one, but now that you have worked your way through this book, perhaps a more detailed discussion will help.

1. *Acknowledge that our child, teen, or grown son or daughter is choosing to ignore the advice and teaching we offer.*

God has no grandchildren, we are taught, and we know that this means each person makes his or her own choice for, or against, God.

The comfort for parents of prodigals is that choices are not eliminated by bad behavior. As with the prodigal of the Bible story, our kids can come home if they wish. But if they choose to remain in the world, we simply turn them over to their loving God (where they have been all along anyway) and trust that He will do what is in their best interest.

Sin is a choice, and so is salvation from that sin. We do not help our kids by pretending that what they are doing is somehow not really of their own choosing.

2. *They can change.*

It may be with difficulty perhaps, but they *can* change. The Bible tells us that reprobates do exist; these are people whom God has given up on. But we are never allowed to evaluate others or encouraged to guess about who might be in that category. Only God decides on reprobates.

Yes, some people will never change. But that reality does

not compromise an opposite reality that *all people can change*. The pain we experience in seeing one of our own kids walk away from God cannot be explained. It is deep, and tears at our very soul. It challenges one's confidence in a loving God.

But my inability to understand what God is doing in the life of my tough kid does not limit his ability to do that work. All I can do is trust. This has always been true, even when I was unaware of it.

3. It is our job as parents to make it as hard as possible for kids to do wrong, and as easy as possible for kids to do right.

We can't do it for them, that's true. But parents can establish an environment in the home that presents options to offspring, options built on the *voluntary* nature of family membership. Years of counseling with adolescents and their parents has convinced me that too many of us are missing an excellent opportunity to teach our kids that the home is our responsibility, and we alone (under God) set the rules.

We may negotiate with our kids if we wish, but there must be a list of absolute "untouchables" that are non-negotiable. Smoking, drinking alcohol, illegal drugs, sex outside marriage, dishonesty—the list goes on. And the list is up to us, mom and dad.

With the exception of legal limitations, no one has the right to tell us what our rules at home should be. The rules we create should encourage good behavior and discourage bad behavior. The Israelite leader, Joshua, declared that, "...as for me and my house, we will serve the Lord" (Joshua 24:15).

The principle that allowed this old man to make such a strong commitment is very simple.

Joshua recognized that to be a member of his family was a choice each person old enough to be considered an adult (even a young adult) could make. Joshua was not promising that each person in that large "tribe" would behave properly, but rather that each one would choose to do so—or choose to leave the family.

This is the attitude I believe God expects us to take with our children *who are old enough to make such a choice.* It is against the law in most states for parents to turn loose a young person under the age of eighteen. But we can find alternate living arrangements for really tough kids who insist on violating house rules. This is not complicated, but it takes a lot of parental strength and fortitude.

4. *We will teach the kids what they need to know.*

Christian parents tend to be very careful to protect their children from the world. No one could criticize this, of course. It is based on love and is well-intentioned. But some of us miss opportunities to really teach the kids *what they need to know* because we are afraid of contaminating them in some way. Again, this protectionism is well-meant, but in most cases, an error.

We must ask ourselves if our desire for protection in the Christian school will compromise our child's education and make them less well-prepared for success in the future. I think this is a real danger with all non-traditional Christian educational systems—and many that are traditional.

In order to avoid presenting temptation to our teenagers, we reject sex education even when presented by a carefully trained and sensitive Christian teacher. Many of us do the same with drug education, AIDS awareness, and so on. I fear that we are inadvertently placing our kids at risk, in that they will have to face the world at some time anyway, and we may be *making them more vulnerable* by keeping them temporarily ignorant.

I know this is controversial. Remember, I am a parent too. But I truly believe many parents who are practicing family isolationism today will pay a heavy price in guilt later on for what their grown children fall victim to. I hope this is not the case with your family, but counselors who work with families as I do will confirm that the world has arrived on our doorstep. We had better get our kids ready to deal with it.

5. *We will not be fooled.*

It is amazing to see how a well-educated, careful, worldly-wise Christian mom or dad can be so easily "conned" by a manipulative kid.

Kids who do this try to convince their parents that if they fail to give in to their kids' unacceptable demands proves the parents don't love or want their children. "You don't trust me. I knew it all along. If you trusted me you would let me go to the party. If you loved me, really loved me, you would let me go."

Heard anything like this lately? It's manipulation, pure and simple. We understand that our kids are going to try this. It seems to be the nature of the beast to try and get what they want from parents in almost *any* way they can. It is up to us to resist these temptations to feel guilty. Our job is to be strong. We should not be vulnerable to accusations that we don't love a child. We know we do. Why then, do many of us fall for this?

So let's toughen up! Let's be like Joshua in our homes. Say "No!" and stick to it. They really do know we love them. After they are grown, they will come back and tell us that they knew we loved them because we did tell them "no." So let's be strong in the Lord.

6. *We will rely on natural consequences to enforce discipline.*

Wise and careful parents will put themselves in the position of being on the child's side when it comes to discipline.

As strange as this may sound (given that it will be the parent who is doing the disciplining), this is what takes place when we employ natural consequences to teach self-discipline. We need to first establish rules that are fair and consistent. Then teach these rules to the children, starting when they are very small. This is very important, because it is much more difficult to correct poor discipline techniques in older children. It's not impossible, but very difficult.

Once the children are taught the rules and understand the consequences for breaking those rules, we should step back and let natural consequences take over. Suppose a ten year old is forbidden to climb the backyard tree higher than the roof line of the house. "This high, and no higher" says the rule, and junior has violated it by climbing to the very top.

Mom gets him down and says "Okay, you know what this means. I'm sorry for you, but no television tonight. I know some of your favorite programs are on, but I'm also sure you can find something constructive to do during that time. I sure hope this doesn't happen again, because I know you enjoy television. But I guess you will have to decide if climbing to the top of the tree is worth giving up television for an evening. It's up to you."

Good parent! This is how natural consequences work with younger kids.

With adolescents and young adults, the consequences may be more significant. They may involving *not* bailing a kid out of trouble with police or school authorities. This may involve *not* begging an employer to give our son or daughter another chance after they have been fired for excessive tardiness on the job.

We can fill in xour own blanks here. Our kids will present us with totally unique varieties of manipulation and begging, but we must be strong! Tough love must be practiced here. We need to be flexible, but not when it involves the absolutes. If we are not sure what the absolutes should be, we can talk to other parents with kids the same age as ours. I guarantee that if our kids hear that we are going to compare notes with the parents of their friends, they will do *anything* they can to stop this from happening. (Let's make sure we do it anyway!)

7. *Acknowledge that our kids are doing what their friends are doing.*

This issue never comes up at the workshops for parents without people getting upset and argumentative. It is so much more comfortable to blame unacceptable behavior on "the wrong crowd" than to recognize that my kid is the problem, not his or her friends. Of course, their friends are not irrelevant. But the critical issue is what attracts my kid or yours to that "bad" group, not how can we eliminate the bad bunch of kids.

We have a choice here, mom and dad. We can insert our collective heads into the sand and feel good for a few weeks or months until the denial bubble breaks, or we can face reality right up front and focus our complete attention on our own kid rather than the group. If we choose the latter option, we have a greatly improved opportunity to help our kid. The choice is ours.

8. *We will not quit.*

Sounds simple, doesn't it? Just don't quit! But the reality, as always, differs from those pious platitudes proffered by porculent preachers. (Sorry about that! I couldn't resist.)

The point is valid though, and it needs emphasis. We do not see Jesus giving up on individual people. It is the belief of most Bible-believing Christians that salvation cannot be lost, that we cannot be put out of the family of God once we are really in it.

So in a sense, we cannot quit with our kids, either. There is nothing to quit. They belong to God anyway, and He is in charge of them, not us. We have a very important role to play of course, but not the most important role.

But encouragement not to quit does not mean that we should allow ourselves to be abused or exploited by our kids. We read about the horrible abuses inflicted on parents by drug-abusing teenagers or grown children, and we shudder. Too many of us do something similar when we give our own prodigals money without their working, or "bail" them out of trouble, or try to get them jobs they can't seem to keep (making us look like fools in the process). We *should* quit being taken advantage of by teenagers or grown children (younger kids need something different), but we should never give up on them. Remember, only God decides who is a reprobate.

9. *We will maintain our testimony even in the darkest days.*

Our kids need stable parents to come home to if they decide to give up their life of sin and return to God.

If we parents let our anger or depression over the "tough" behavior of our kids distract us from what God wants us to do in this life, they will not have a "home base" if and when they need one. I don't mean we should always be prepared to take our grown kids back into the home. But we need to demonstrate for them that we can do all things through Christ who strengthens us—even if it means maintaining our sanity in the face of the worst possible behavior from them.

Imagine having a teenager or adult child in prison. Imagine learning that a nineteen-year-old daughter has become a prostitute in another city, or that a son or daughter has "come out of the closet" and announced his or her homosexuality. Or a fourteen-year-old daughter announcing to us that she is pregnant and doesn't know who the father is. We could go on and on with examples, but these are not examples.

I have heard all of these terrible realities from Christian parents in the counseling office. I've heard all of these, and many, many others. It may be that only those Christian parents who have faced these terrible dark valleys can fully appreciate what it means to acknowledge that their children belong to God and are in his ultimate care. Perhaps only they can fully understand that we are stewards for just a little while, doing for God what He has ordained us to do. But don't quit! Don't let a rebellious son or daughter chase you away from church.

I can recall a Wednesday evening prayer service a few years ago when we were struggling with a rebellious sixteen-year-old son. Linda wept all the way through the service. She wept—and I boiled. The situation was resolved, and our son is doing fine. *But we had to maintain our relationship with the Lord during those dark days.*

Today, our son is in his mid-twenties, married with two sons, and has commented to us more than a few times how much he was impressed that we did not chase after him, begging and pleading to do right, but just kept on keeping on. Don't quit!

Onward and upward

Parenting is not terminal. Being a parent is, of course, but the work of parenting will not go on for life. Welcome the "empty nest," mom and dad. Linda and I have found it terrific! We take vacations by ourselves now (after 31 years!). We have time for each other that we have not experienced since the children came along.

Onward and upward. *There is life after children.* New ministries await. There are new opportunities to serve and glorify God with our labor. We may have more money to share with missionaries and other good works now that the kids are on their own. We can employ the energy we once gave to 24-hour-a-day parenting to helping young families in the church. And we will have time to sit and think, to just "meditate" on life and God and what this all means.

Onward and upward, mom and dad.

Tough kids need not ruin your life or cost you your marriage or your testimony. Tough kids need tough parents like us who can do everything possible to make it hard for the kids to do wrong, and everything possible to make it easy for them to do right.

Onward and upward, mom and dad. God bless you!

Other books by Dr. David Miller

Single Moms, Single Dads
Help & Hope for the One Parent Family

Help! I'm Not A Perfect Parent
Overcoming the Guilty-Parent Syndrome

A Parents' Guide To Adolescents
Understanding Your Teenager

Parent Power
Godly Influence in an Age of Weakness

Christian Parenting
T O D A Y

☐ **YES,** please enter a subscription to *Christian Parenting Today* under my name at the address specified below.

☐ 1 year (6 issues) of *Christian Parenting Today* for only $16.97.

☐ 2 years (12 issues) of *Christian Parenting Today* for only $24.97. **Save $10.43!**

NAME _____

ADDRESS _____

CITY _____ STATE _____ ZIP _____

For fast service with a credit card call
1-800-238-2221.

☐ Payment enclosed

☐ Bill me

Outside U.S. add $5.40 per year in U.S. funds only (GST included).

B2C21

Christian Parenting Today
P. O. Box 850
Sisters, OR 97759
1-800-238-2221